LEAD LIKE A WOMAN

Tales From the Trenches

Brought to you
by Andrea Heuston

Featuring 10 Inspiring
Women Entrepreneurs

Lead Like a Woman

Published by Prominence Publishing

www.Prominencepublishing.com

ISBN: 978-1-988925-98-1

For all the women who have ever been told they are "too much."

They're wrong - you're leaders with grit, passion, and tenacity.

Table of Contents

FOREWORD

By Karen Austin

I AM A WOMAN WHO DOESN'T believe much in coincidence, so I wasn't surprised (although I laughed) when I sat down to write this foreword and realized it was International Women's Day (a global day celebrating the social, economic, cultural, and political achievements of women). In that moment, mask mandates were ending, men and women were returning to the workplace, and Spring was beginning to look like a real possibility after two very long winters for all of us.

Yet across the world, so far from my home office in Ohio, mothers in Ukraine dropped off their children for safekeeping with relatives and friends in other countries—and then returned to actual trenches to fight for theirs.

I was reflecting on that—this non-coincidence of writing about women leading from the trenches on a day that celebrates us—

and gazing out the window at the still bare trees moving gently in the wind. It had rained hard the night before, and a half dozen girl robins (so fat and healthy this year!) plucked worms from a damp ditch to take back to their nests.

As I watched them, I thought, you know, sometimes we women dig our own trenches and sometimes the storms dig them for us. What you'll find on the pages of this extraordinary book are stories of both types —and the lessons that come from laboring in them.

When Andrea Heuston, who is the creator of the Lead Like a Woman podcast and the instigator of this book, asked me to write the foreword, I asked her why, of course. She said, "Because you'll know what to say."

Unless you're one of the three women with whom I've worked intimately and whose tales are included in this book, you'll have no idea who I am. I am a writer, an author, a storyteller, an enthusiastic student of leadership. Perhaps most importantly for the purposes of this foreword, I am a keen and dedicated observer and supporter of women.

What I want to say is this: at nearly 65 years young, I've been observing for a good long while. I've seen some ugly tear each-other-down behavior. You'll see some of that in this book. I've watched us work shoulder to shoulder (with and without pads) in our collective deep trench—you know, the one the world STILL keeps trying to fill in behind as we go. So, we have to dig it again. And again.

And we do because we're women. To expand on the war metaphor conjured by the term "in the trenches" and the actual war our Ukraine sisters are engaged in, I want to say to anyone reading this and those strong women vulnerable enough to share their tales on these pages, "keep digging, warrior." And by warrior, I simply mean that fierce feminine energy that keeps you lifting the shovel.

One final thing. These stories and these women who tell them, will remind you that you're not alone. That every insecurity you've had, every imposter syndrome tale you've told yourself, every conversation you've had with that woman in your head who tells you you're not good enough (I stopped hanging out with that bitch decades ago, btw) is a lie.

FOREWORD

This book was created and curated by women who lift up other women by choice, who make a habit and practice of it, who use their hard-earned lessons to teach, and their wisdom to nurture.

I know you'll meet yourself here, and make some new friends and colleagues, as well.

Yours in the dig,

Karen Austin
March 8, 2022
Westerville, Ohio

INTRODUCTION

"Never, ever mistake her silence for weakness.
Remember that sometimes the air stills
before the onset of a hurricane."
—*Nikita Gill*

By Andrea Heuston

THANK YOU FOR JOINING US. I'm excited you're here. It's been a long road to this book. It's been both scary and fun.

You see, two years ago, as the pandemic was in its early throes of uncertainty and fear, I birthed a new podcast. I use that term – birthed – because it felt like a new beginning, something big, something I'd wanted to do for a long time, and it became my baby. The Lead Like a Woman Show has reached tens of thousands of people so far. I know it's making a difference in women's lives. It's helping them find and own their power as leaders, community members, and as warriors. Because we're all warriors, battling daily against preconceived notions, societal norms, and family of origin traditions.

Through the show, I have met, interviewed, and even become friends with the most incredible women. These women lead every day—in business, in their communities, in their families. They face issues head-on. They figure out solutions, they stumble, they fall. But they rise with new information, with new muscles, with new power.

From the podcast, I realized that these women all have powerful stories to share. They have lessons learned the hard way, overcoming huge hurdles. But each one of them has a positive attitude and has been able to turn their lessons into effective momentum for their businesses and their personal lives. It's been so impactful for me, and for my listeners.

Within these pages, you will get a chance to learn from our mistakes. Mistakes that range from poor hiring to imposter syndrome; from using the word NO as motivation to learning that it's okay to need other people. You'll understand how expectations can get in our way but also bring clarity. You'll have a chance to face unknowns, grapple with failure, and become the master of your own miracles. It's exciting for me to be able to help share stories of leadership and learning to really own who you are as a person, as a leader, as a woman.

There's so much good stuff in this book. *Lead Like a Woman: Tales from the Trenches* is full of real: real stories, real leaders, real women. It's heartbreaking and heart soothing. It takes you from mistakes to success and in between again. We are daughters, mothers, partners, friends, and leaders. But mostly we're warriors learning to use failure as a stepping stone to our next great achievement.

Enjoy the journey!

CHAPTER 1

Hire Slow and Fire Fast: How I Learned – *The Hard Way* – To Heed This Advice

By Andrea Heuston

YOU KNOW THE SAYING, "Hire slow, fire fast?" I've learned the hard way — many times — that I should adhere to that advice. When I first started my business, I was a "solopreneur." I was a freelancer, contractor, independent designer. I loved it, until I didn't.

Learning the Hard Way

Ten years into running a one-person show, I had too much work and too many clients to run my business alone. I incorporated the company and began hiring employees. My first hire was recommended by two people I greatly respected. These two people didn't know each other and had never crossed paths. I interviewed Jenny and asked the questions I thought I should I ask. We discussed the role, which was a hybrid of office manager and personal assistant. In hindsight, I'm not sure our personalities were a good match, but she was recommended by two of my contacts, a good friend, and a long-time colleague! So, I hired her.

At the same time, I asked one of my best friends, Sharon, to be my bookkeeper. She was a bookkeeper by trade and had worked as one for many years before starting her family. She had only just decided to stay at home to raise her children and wanted a part-time gig. She had been the maid of honor at my wedding, and I trusted her implicitly. She was, at the time, taking a hiatus from the corporate world and welcomed the work.

I thought I was set! I had two, strong female employees who could help me grow my business from a one-woman shop to a creative solutions provider for enterprise clients. I hired a business coach, I joined a peer group, I got a CPA, and a lawyer. I did all the things I thought I was supposed to do to create momentum and growth in my business.

It became clear fairly early on that Jenny was not happy in her role. We were working out of my house at the time, using the home office and dining room as a base. We hired a designer, and went in search of office space, but until we found it, we shared a table for a desk in my home. Part of Jenny's job was to take some personal chores off my plate — pick up dry cleaning, schedule meetings, grab my lunch, prepare my notes. Things that all took time away from meeting with clients and landing new business. She complained constantly about these "chores" as she called them. She hated the personal assistant part of her role. And she liked to commiserate with others about her misery, so she chose Sharon.

Sharon was, in my mind, a fabulous bookkeeper. She balanced the accounts, kept track of taxes, paid the bills, and created budgets for me. I didn't have to do any of the financial tasks. I just brought in the work, made sure it was done to my high standards, invoiced the clients, and signed the checks. I never looked at the bank account, I never questioned the checks I signed. Why would I? Sharon was someone I trusted. We were *best friends*, for god's sake!

Jenny and Sharon formed a bond. Jenny needed someone to complain to — about me — and Sharon was the perfect person. They chatted often via Microsoft Messenger, and Jenny saved all of the messages in a file on her computer.

As the company grew, we hired additional employees. A few designers, a few contractors, a new executive assistant for me. We moved into an office building, and I felt like we'd finally become a "real" business. Jenny took over the office management and administrative duties that came with the new space and bigger staff. But she was clearly still not happy. Adding to her unhappiness was the fact that she wasn't doing her job well, and I had started to question her value within the company. She was often late, and she had overstated her skillset. I created a Performance Improvement Plan, talked with her about what she needed to do to stay with the company, and gave her 30 days to improve her skills and attitude.

After 30 days, it was clear that Jenny would not be able to complete the Performance Improvement Plan. When I finally found the strength to terminate Jenny's employment, I called my lawyer — the lawyer that Jenny had found for the company and had created a relationship with. I had never fired someone before. I had laid people off in a former job, but never fired anyone for cause. My lawyer walked me through everything. I had a plan.

After firing Jenny, I confiscated her computer. On the computer were several things that should never have been on a work-issued computer. Amongst her many personal files, I found a folder full of message transcripts from conversations she'd had with Sharon. The messages were incriminating. Jenny complaining — at length — about me. And Sharon, trying to console her, offered things like a spa weekend with her girlfriend, at the company's expense. Sharon offered her many things — from meals to massages to the spa weekend. All at my expense. Literally, at my expense. She instructed Jenny to pad her expense reports and Sharon would have me sign the checks. Which I did, of course. Without any question in my mind.

Sharon never stole money herself, but she led and encouraged Jenny's transgressions. And since I had no idea that I should be looking at my numbers, reviewing expense reports, checking the bank accounts, I let it happen. The money lost totaled thousands and thousands of dollars.

That evening, I read and reread the transcripts then sat at my desk and cried for hours. I confronted Sharon and fired her immediately. My husband had to load the kids into their car seats and come to get me at the office. I was too distraught to even drive the 7 miles home and I learned a lesson: to understand and pay attention to my finances. But I still had more lessons to learn about hiring and firing.

Still Learning

The next week, I started interviewing office managers. I interviewed three in one day, and two the next. On the second day of interviewing, I had a candidate in my office and our intranet went down. We couldn't access our server or work on client projects without it. The candidate I was interviewing took over. She assessed the issue, called a friend in IT who walked her through several processes, and fixed the problem. She was a referral from one of my trusted contract designers. I hired her on the spot. What could go wrong?

Well, I never checked her references. If I had done so, I would have found out she'd been in jail in another state. I likely would have unearthed that she was unstable and possibly violent. After working for the company for a few weeks, she ended up throwing a chair at a contract employee. The contracting firm threatened to sue my company. Again, I called my lawyer. He advised me to have another person present when firing her. I brought my husband in, who works in Human Resources. I fired her and she signed a separation agreement. But she wouldn't go quietly. It took weeks to finally have her out of my company, and out of my hair. Another hard lesson learned.

Sometimes it Takes Many Lessons

A few years later, when one of my favorite designers decided to leave the company for a corporate job, we spent a lot of time and resources hiring a new associate creative director. We searched far and wide, looked at personal referrals, and interviewed each candidate multiple times. I was trying hard to hire smarter. I thought I had learned all I needed to know about hiring well. We ended up hiring Matthew. He was a great interview.

Two weeks after hiring Matthew, I ended up in a coma for 17 days. After coming out of the coma, it took me over six months to come back to work in a nearly full-time capacity. When I started working with Matthew, I realized quickly that he was not the person I thought we had hired. He was condescending, he told me constantly that I was a horrible designer. I started to believe him. He was demeaning to the design team and a very difficult person to work with. While I had been out of the office, ill, he had started telling the team he was going to be running the company soon, not me. He undermined me, undermined the team, and argued with the project managers. He did, however, charm the clients.

One day, one of my senior designers came into my office to resign. She was an incredibly talented individual, easy to work with, creative, and fun. She was leaving because she could no longer work with Matthew. She had gotten hives because the anxiety of coming to the office each day and working with her manager had become too toxic. She could no longer tolerate the culture in the office. That was the day I decided to fire him.

This time when I called my lawyer, he offered to come to my office to help. We created a letter of separation, giving Matthew compensation for not taking any of our clients with him. He decided not to sign the document and walked away with three of our major clients. They all came back within a year.

Throughout the 25+ years I've owned a business, I've had many opportunities to learn, and so many of them the hard way. I hired someone who was fantastic with clients, but toxic to the culture. I caught another employee doing hard drugs at work, and others who just couldn't perform their jobs at the level needed. It's never easy to fire someone. And I hate it every time. Another CEO once said to me, "There's no benefit for me to fire someone." I believe he's right. Sometimes, however, it must be done, and sometimes I must be the one to do it.

Hiring and firing are my least favorite parts of my job. Therefore, I no longer hire people myself. Rather, I have my team do it. I am the very last person to interview a candidate. Our business operations manager vets each candidate before sending them on to the hiring team. That team then interviews each candidate. After that, if someone makes it through the process, they are presented to me. I have the trump card — I can say no if I don't think they'd be a good fit for the culture or for our client base.

However, if my team has done all the legwork and they highly recommend someone, I usually tend to listen.

Firing someone is even harder. I haven't had to fire anyone in quite some time. The last person to leave my company retired after 12 years with the firm. I like to think it's because I've become better at hiring. It also has to do with culture and creating an environment where people are both allowed to fail and are celebrated for being themselves. A positive corporate culture is vital for the success of the company. Employees will stay where they feel empowered and appreciated.

I really do not know everything about hiring and firing, nor do I pretend to, even after 25+ years in business. But I do know that keeping talent is important and maintaining a strong company culture promotes productivity and happy, dedicated employees. And happy employees tend to lead to satisfied clients who return again and again.

Making the Lessons Stick

Here are three things I always reflect on when it comes to hiring and firing:

1. It's important to be transparent. When you are hiring a new employee, transparency in the team, people, and processes helps them feel welcome. When letting someone go, being transparent about your concerns ensures that the person leaving understands why they are being let go.

2. Consider the company's future business needs and whether the potential employee or the employee in question has the necessary skillset and mindset to help the organization grow.

3. Don't rely solely on your own observations about a potential employee or an employee that may need to be let go. Seek input from other trusted colleagues. Do not make the decision to hire or fire in a silo.

Team culture can make or break a company and people are the key ingredient to success. Through transparency, teamwork, and communications you can build and maintain a strong team. Just remember, when hiring and firing, you can always teach skills, but you cannot teach character.

About the Author

Andrea Heuston is the Founder and CEO of Artitudes Design Inc. and has been in the creative tech industry for over 30 years. Artitudes is a creative communications solutions provider, helping clients communicate with their audiences in an impactful way. Andrea is a respected business leader, speaker, coach and entrepreneur who is sought after as a board member and a Keynote speaker. She is a prolific voice on women's and leadership topics in the workforce—Which has given rise to her success as a LinkedIn Social network influencer.

In 2020, she started her podcast "The Lead Like a Woman Show" focusing on empowering women leaders to empower others through topical discussions and interviews with female leaders. She is passionate about helping to close the gender gap for women in business.

Her book, *Stronger on the Other Side* was written to empower women with the power to choose their own path. When she's not busy with speaking, writing, hosting, and creative projects, you can find her walking on the beach with her family and two Australian Shepherds.

Connect with Andrea:

http://AndreaHeuston.com/
http://LeadLikeAWoman.biz/
LinkedIn: AndreaHeuston

CHAPTER 2

Learning to Lead Like Me

By Lisa Liguori

WHEN I WAS JUST A TEENAGER, my dad asked me to head up a project to sell a ninety-five-thousand-square-foot commercial building owned by his company. I still vividly remember that short conversation. I was sitting at the kitchen table, as I often did after school, pulling out my English homework.

My dad: "Would you sell the Cabot Drive building for me?"

Me: "But Dad, I'm a kid. I don't know how to sell buildings."

My dad: "I know, but you're smart; you'll figure it out."

To my own surprise, I did figure it out. It was my first taste of business leadership, my first shot at trying to be like my hero, my dad.

Most of us can point to people in our lives who inspired us to reach for leadership: a sports coach or a favorite boss who showed us the impact a good leader can have, someone who made us want to emulate them.

For me, that inspiration was my dad.

When I was a little girl, my favorite thing was to visit him at his office: a big, white industrial building with an orange stripe around the top, where he led more than 2,000 employees at National Pen Corporation, a manufacturer of promotional products. I loved watching my dad greet his coworkers and interact with his staff, all of whom he treated like close friends. If he saw someone who needed to learn to save money, he'd offer to match their savings. If they struggled with their weight, he would help them set goals to achieve good health. If they were in a tight spot and needed legal help, he would foot the bill for an attorney. He was constantly giving of himself to improve the lives of those around him.

In my eyes, he was the ideal of what a leader should be. So, when faced with choosing a college major, I studied business. I wanted to stay close and follow his every move. But no two people are the same, and I was setting myself up to measure my own success against his very tall shadow.

After working for the family business for a time, I ventured out on my own. The first small business I launched was Elite Students of America. We used data to match aspiring high school students with colleges that matched their criteria. I loved incorporating my first business, choosing a name, designing a logo, and conducting interviews to hire my first employees — but the venture collapsed within a year.

I tried again with a new concept. It also was unprofitable, and I repeated the pattern several times. With each experience of what I considered failure, I grew more hopeless that I could ever build a fraction of what my dad had.

I wanted to believe that, as my dad always told me, everything I did (including starting unprofitable ventures) was laying the groundwork for future success. But all I felt was self-doubt. I continued to hold up my dad as the standard by which I measured success, even though that bar felt impossible to reach. If this was the path to becoming a great leader, I was failing.

In 2004, our family listed the 57-year-old pen company my dad and grandfather built for sale. I re-engaged with the family business to help my dad and the management team pitch to groups of potential buyers. It was an exhilarating experience to work with such an incredibly tight-knit group of people at an exciting time in the business. I was, as always, in awe of all that my dad had built. I thought building something and then seeing the fruits of that hard work alongside a close, loving team with a rich history was one of the most joyful moments of my life, and the pinnacle that any businessperson could experience.

That liquidity event, the result of my dad's hard work for so many years, meant that my dad needed to re-envision his career. With all his energy, purpose, and creativity, there was not a chance he was going to retire. And I was excited when he invited me to start a new company with him.

For the next 16 years, we ran a direct investment fund together, buying companies on behalf of our family. For the most part, we made purchase decisions together and my dad took the point in communicating with our portfolio companies.

About six years into our partnership, an opportunity came up that both my dad and I agreed would be a good learning experience for me: one of the distressed companies we purchased needed a CEO to turn things around. This was the chance I'd been waiting for—an opportunity to become the leader my dad had taught me to be.

Sadly, I struggled again, and that experience was one of the most difficult and frustrating of my career. The employees I inherited resisted the changes I tried to initiate, and I felt my inability to enroll them was due entirely to my incompetence. The issues didn't stop with the legacy employees. My first five key hires all either quit or I had to fire them. While striving to be a beloved leader like my dad, I was panned in exit interviews.

I read every business management book I could find, worked with executive coaches, and took advice from fellow business owners. Yet, instead of engendering love and respect as my dad had with his people from the very early days of his business, I was disliked and unable to inspire the group. I felt this proved my inadequacy as a leader.

I also struggled to build sales, and without new revenue coming in, I racked up company debt equal to the amount we had paid to acquire the business, essentially doubling the purchase price.

I put in long hours thinking maybe hard work was the difference between the success my dad had and the results I was getting. The more things I tried without success, the more and more I felt personally flawed and being in that mental space wore me down. I was not taking care of my health and grew increasingly negative. I didn't like who I was becoming.

I stepped down as CEO but continued co-managing the direct investment company with my father. I was crushed that I couldn't be like my hero, but comforted myself by spending time with him, my favorite person. We met in his office to discuss portfolio companies, took weekly walks around the business park, and did fun things like play tennis and race cars.

Then in July of 2020, my dad, who had always meticulously cared for his health, was diagnosed with brain cancer. Suddenly, our family, which was already my priority, became the only thing that mattered. My mom, siblings, and I spent the last seven months of my dad's life savoring him.

Before he died, my dad — with my mom and siblings' blessings — anointed me to continue running the family business. My dad expressed great confidence in my ability and he felt tremendous peace knowing that he was leaving me at the helm. While that was deeply affirming and a great honor, I thought my dad had more confidence in me than I deserved. He had always been my biggest fan and his estimation of me was great.

But I looked at my track record of starting businesses that didn't make money. I thought of how often I had dabbled in the business without finding a clear and unique way to contribute. I thought of how many employees had left me and I compared that with my dad's team. When my father proposed moving his company from Florida to California, 100% of his staff agreed to relocate across the country to stay with him!

While I felt unworthy of the responsibility, I wanted to support my family.

On February 9th, 2021, my precious dad died.

A month later, I found myself in his office, with boxes of my own things and boxes of his. I would box up some of the contents of a single drawer in my dad's desk every few weeks and carefully store them while moving in some of the contents from my old desk. I feared my presence might push out his presence, which I desperately wanted to preserve.

While I knew I had the support of my staff, the reality was that they had signed up to be on my dad's team, not mine. And as the sole family representative, I felt the gaping hole my dad's physical departure created. I was comforted during that time by the example my dad set for me with the way he lived his life.

Ready or not, I quickly faced decisions of large financial consequence. Historically, my dad and I would have made those decisions together. I always had a backstop because someone smarter, more experienced, and more confident than me was right by my side as we navigated business challenges.

I wanted a playbook for how to navigate this new chapter of life that had come too soon and with very little warning. I wanted to articulate how my dad led so that I could follow the script and emulate him to the best of my ability in every move I made. To do this, I started journaling about my dad's amazing traits as a leader. I read notes people had written about him and watched video messages his friends had sent to pay tribute to him in an event we put on before he became ill.

People shared that my dad had always encouraged them to try new things — to experiment, and to not worry about the results. He told them they'd only learn by trying. They talked about how present he was as a listener. They shared how my dad was secure enough to give another man a big hug and tell him that he loved him, and they disclosed how at difficult times in their lives, he had quietly offered financial support that relieved their stress.

I wanted to translate those descriptions into an instruction manual for my new role. I didn't want to lose any piece of learning he had taught me. Fortunately, having been so close to my dad, I felt as if I knew how he would have thought, and what he would have done in almost every situation. So, each time I came to a fork in the road I would ask myself, "What would Dad do?"

There was one problem with my approach, though. What had worked for my dad wasn't working the same way for me. For example, my dad had a certain set of expert advisors, and he trusted these people and was pleased with their work. But I felt unhappy with some of those same people's performances. One consultant was so unresponsive that it took an average of six emails and several weeks before he would reply to each issue that arose.

Since my assessment of these people deviated from my dad's, I asked myself, "Why were these people good enough for my dad but not for me? Am I too demanding? Is this why dad was so beloved, and I am not?" I grappled with why I couldn't make the team function while it helped my dad thrive.

I constantly sought affirmation that I was on the right path. I would be in a video meeting and hear a business partner say something I thought was unfair. My heart would beat faster, and my leg would start bouncing frantically to dissipate nervous energy. I would look at my team's faces to see if anyone else had the same reaction. I expected them to be as apoplectic as I was. But most often, they didn't show any signs of surprise or alarm; so I would second guess myself. I thought if other smart people didn't see it the way I did, I must be off base. After all, I was not a good leader like my dad had been, so I was probably wrong.

To compound the problem, any time I made a decision that was different from what my dad had done in the past, I felt by definition it was an inferior decision. Others on my team were reinforcing that notion, continuing to make decisions based on what they thought my dad would have done. After key decisions I made, they commented on whether they thought my dad would have made the same, or a different, decision. One even expressed disappointment when I made decisions that differed.

I felt trapped.

To find and fix the problem, I joined a peer group composed of entrepreneurial female business leaders (that ironically, I didn't feel I belonged in). Every time we met over Zoom, coffee cups and smoothies in hand, I learned more about how each of the ten women led her respective organization. I saw how some led with a lot of heart and emotion, shedding sad tears when talking about the employee who left or happy tears when expressing pride in the way her team pulled together. I heard some women describe a very hands-on approach while others were master delegators. I watched more observant leaders sit quietly taking in the conversation until they had something poignant and powerful to say, while others engaged in lively debate that developed ideas. Despite the many differences in the women, each was a powerful leader.

One day, I was on one of my weekly hikes with my friend and coach, Jessica Zemple. As we walked along a beautiful coastal trail in San Diego, I shared with her my disappointment in myself for wanting more from people than my dad had required and told her about my angst when I arrived at different decisions than my dad would have made.

Jessica posed a question I had never even considered, "What if the decisions you are making are not actually inferior to those of your dad, but rather made with even more perspective because your dad has given you a head start?" She painted a picture of my dad putting me on his shoulders so that I could see far into the distance with great perspective.

That metaphor allowed me to see that my dad and I had different perspectives – not better or worse. With that reframing of the situation, I started allowing for the possibility that my judgment and perspective were sound. I started listening a little bit more closely to my instincts and professional judgment.

I started to wonder if the question I should be asking myself was not, "How can I lead exactly like dad did?" but rather, "How can I take the learning I gained from dad and use it to lead like the best version of myself?" My sense is that I can be much more successful by becoming the best version of myself than by trying to emulate my role model. Not only would this be more effective and help me serve to my highest potential, but I think it would also be my dad's wish.

A test of my new resolve came when I had to decide whether to keep funding one of our portfolio companies. The business was hemorrhaging cash and we had been bankrolling the expenses month after month. The founder of that company is a family friend whom my dad loved and had great hopes of helping to build a successful business. Turning off the funding meant allowing one of my dad's dreams to go unfulfilled. That was painful. Stopping the loans also meant risking damage to a friendship important to my dad. On top of that stress, my CFO urged me to continue funding several hundred thousand dollars more. He added, "I think your dad intended to."

I agonized over the decision. But this time, I could not stomach ignoring my judgment. I concentrated on my responsibility to protect my family's assets and made the decision to close the company down. As difficult as that was, I experienced peace and a feeling of empowerment as soon as I made the decision.

It turned out to be the responsible choice.

With each decision I make, I gain a little bit more confidence that I have an internal compass I can trust.

I've realized that despite all the theories I learned in business school, the formulas in the management books I devoured, and the axioms that leadership professors espouse as the "enlightened" way to lead, there is no one model for exceptional leadership. My dad and I might look at the same situation in a boardroom and make different decisions.

I'm finally okay with that.

As I spend time with many successful CEOs, I see amazing leaders question their worth, and I wonder how they could miss seeing their incredible strengths. Questioning our value is not just rampant but also insidious because it robs us of the energy we could invest in advancing our dreams. Bandwidth that's used for worrying about our rightful place could be harnessed for contributing our gifts to making the world a better place.

Today, almost a year after I moved into the corner office, I am trying to honor my dad's legacy through a different path than I originally envisioned. I still reflect heavily on what I think he would have said or done about every major decision. But I am also spending time listening to my inner voice for my reactions, intuition, and thoughts. I do that by journaling, taking short nature walks to contemplate, and talking things through with my friends and advisors. I weigh my own opinion in addition to the others I gather.

The world misses out when any one of us doesn't bring our full selves to the boardroom. I am working to liberate myself from the guilt that I'm not someone else. I've decided it's time to lead like me.

About the Author

Some of Lisa Liguori's most unique experiences have been swimming with tiger sharks in Fiji, photographing giraffes in South Africa, and piloting a small plane with her husband, David. Though she loves to travel, home is her "happy place" because it's where she can be close to family and never miss a Sunday dinner.

By day Lisa runs a venture capital firm in San Diego; but even in the boardroom, she prefers jeans and flip flops over suits and heels. One of her favorite roles is as a philanthropist, directing her private foundation.

In her spare time, she loves watching personal development videos, cooking plant-based recipes, and getting together with friends for game nights.

While Lisa has many interests, she believes her calling is running the Advice Column Podcast. There she brings people together to share their life-experiences. Through that exchange she helps people to feel connected and accelerate their personal growth.

Though she battles shyness, Lisa revels in the adventure of life and dreams of one day participating in a flash mob dance. (Please call her if you are organizing one!)

Connect with Lisa:

www.AdviceColumn.com
lisa@advicecolumn.com
Phone: 858.449.6495

CHAPTER 3

Imposter Abroad

By Shenandoah Davis

BUILDING ONE OF THE COUNTRY'S largest nanny agencies had, I thought, prepared me for just about any issue that could come up. We have worked with families from every industry, background, and walk of life. The one commonality these families all share is that their level of success is far more than most people ever imagine for themselves. These families can be inspirational and intimidating to work with at the same time. For them, finding the person who will join their team to support, educate, and raise their children as both a partner and employee is an incredibly sensitive and important task —and one that I have never taken lightly. Without violating any of the thousands of non-disclosure agreements I've signed over the years, I'll share that we've dealt with private investigators, defensive driving courses, political and sports scandals, children shooting their nannies with bows and arrows, and the run-of-the-mill gossip headlines that are, unfortunately, the only time up to this point that nannies appeared in the press. Glibly, after navigating through a whirlwind of situations, conflicts, and international incidents, I thought Adventure Nannies had weathered every flavor of storm — of course, I was incorrect.

It was March of 2020 — almost exactly to the date that, four years before, I had joined a small start-up as their third employee. Adventure Nannies had grown significantly, particularly for the last couple of years. Our team had grown from three to 10 people, our revenue had increased sevenfold, and we felt positioned for greatness. Nevertheless, I decided to take a few weeks' break (the most extended break I had planned since joining the company) to return to my other profession before joining the domestic staffing industry — my career as a touring musician. My love of songwriting and performing had, at that point, spanned nearly 15 years, three full-length albums, and over one thousand shows across the US, Europe, Japan, and New Zealand. But it had taken a backseat as I stepped into a role that, imposter syndrome aside, I was vastly unqualified for in any sense of the word. My resume (not that I had ever made one) had a variety of barista, server, and bartender positions on it — primarily short-lived for when I was in between tours or attempting to refill my bank account before another gratifying, but never financially successful, tour around the world.

My first few paychecks went towards a triple-digit list of business books I was sure I desperately needed to read and re-read. I had never been a particularly good student, but I immersed myself in a wide range of topics — how to start, run, and scale a business, the complex history of domestic staffing and its roots in systemic racism and slavery, the unique challenges faced by high net worth and high-profile families, and even how to buy a house and get approved for a mortgage as an "unwed woman." (Yes, the state of Washington felt the need to clarify that on my mortgage paperwork.) However useful for my role at Adventure Nannies, none of the information translated into anything to compose music about. Pitchfork had heralded the most recent album I had released as "pitch-perfect chamber pop," but I did not imagine a follow-up with songs about shopping for liability insurance or what insightful questions to ask a nanny in a job interview would be met with the same accolades. However, a friend offered to book a string of shows in Germany and Belgium (17 shows in 21 days), and my partner and I had not yet been to Europe together. The idea of combining musical performances with a romantic sightseeing trip sounded fabulous. Knowing that the trip would almost definitely lose money — as most tours do for indie musicians — and serve as a tax write-off appealed to my newly-found sense of business acumen.

After months of planning and ensuring Adventure Nannies would run smoothly in my absence, my partner and I boarded a flight to Hamburg on March 11, 2020. We did not know that a travel ban between the US and Europe would be issued while we were mid-flight — we found out quickly when our plane touched down in Paris, and my business partner, employees, family, and friends urged us to come home while we still could. We had a long layover, and I had never been to Paris, so we took the Paris Metro into the city to see Notre Dame cathedral under construction and eat croissants while we weighed our options. We decided to roll the dice and continue our trip upon returning to the airport, even upon seeing the chaos from the announcement. We arrived in Hamburg, picked up a rental car, and slept for a few hours before heading to Berlin for my first show. Unfortunately, while driving to Berlin, the show was canceled. The following day, we found out all my shows were canceled.

Schools began closing and offices shut down. Adventure Nannies was working with quite a few families on their nanny searches at the time. We decided to give every client the option of putting their search on hold while most of the world's infrastructure disintegrated due to COVID-19, without a clear understanding of what it was, how it was transmitted, and how long it would last. Overnight, we went from 32 clients to four, with no idea when they might be returning or how long this pandemic would last.

As the two of us continued to move around Germany in a bit of a trance, trying to navigate restrictions and best practices that shifted day-by-day and state-by-state, I was quickly pulled back into the office. Adventure Nannies had grown quickly, and we had chosen growth over pulling profit at every possible turn for the last few years. As a result, we only had enough in the bank to cover eight weeks of expenses. I remember my placement director Christina, who was out on parental leave as she had just given birth to her beautiful daughter, texting me to see what she could do to help the business. I called her while pacing in front of the Spree River, thanked her for thinking of us, and let her know the single thing she could do to be most beneficial to the business would be to stay on parental leave, since we were unsure if there would be a job for her to return to in six weeks. (Note: in hindsight, I am acutely aware that this was possibly not my finest or most inspirational moment as a boss, ever.)

A routine built out of necessity and chaos ensued in the days that followed. I would update the nCov2019 tracker app every 30 seconds, watching the numbers climb dramatically worldwide. For the business, I built spreadsheets to understand what expenses could be cut and where the benchmark for eliminating them could be to stretch out what little money we had in reserves for as long as possible. I tried to research if a CEO could furlough themselves and legally volunteer to continue working at the business. We would move hotels every couple of days in an effort to 'feel safer' and fall asleep staring at the air conditioner unit growling and whirring in our ceiling, wondering if it was a potential source of the mystery virus. We walked through cities that felt nearly abandoned and ate at least one doner kebab every day. At a friend's apartment in Hamburg, we went onto a balcony to clang pots and pans to praise our brave first responders, only to realize we were the only ones doing it and perhaps we had gotten the night wrong. The days sort of smeared together and we stopped counting them — the only thing that changed was that each day, thousands of people got sick and more things shut down.

I have constantly rolled my eyes at the phrase "imposter syndrome" and considered it to be a phrase reserved for the most privileged, whitest, straightest, most buttoned-up folks in our society. This term belongs in an inspirational MLM speech or some motivational course sad people pay for out of desperation. I never considered myself having imposter syndrome — because I was simply an imposter. I had no business running a business. I went to school to earn an opera degree, which I barely squeaked through with an embarrassingly low GPA. I moved from Colorado to Seattle, became a songwriter, released three full-length albums I wrote, and toured the world, playing over 500 shows. I did not make money — certainly never enough to both pay my rent and continue investing in merchandise, touring, paying other musicians, or recording. That wasn't on my radar as something that would really ever be possible. On paper, I was successful as a DIY artist: with the press, the accolades, performing with many of my musical heroes, performing at Folsom Prison and other venues around the country. I have the tour posters to prove it (all of which are currently molding in my 100-year-old garage). I remember turning 29 in the small ferry town of Picton on the south island of New Zealand and spending a few hours sitting on a dock in a pair of ripped-up jeans that hadn't been washed in a few weeks, staring at the Tara O Te Marama mountains and contemplating the 11 years that had passed since I had health insurance, the less-than-$500 I had to my name, and trying to calculate out what accommodations and food would cost for the three humans I had in tow with me on this tour. How many dinners were provided for in the few nights to come? How late could I get away with paying my rent at home in Seattle? What would happen if a single show got canceled, or we didn't sell enough CDs (yes, CDs) at the shows, or didn't result in the couple of hundred dollars we had come to rely on from passing a hat or similar vessel around to the kind constituents at our nightly performances? What would we eat, and where would we sleep?

I had worked my fingers to the bone at Adventure Nannies — it was the first job I ever had that felt like there was a tangible, visceral, positive response to hard work and long hours.

Unfortunately, there was always a self-proclaimed sacrifice to make and an invisible endpoint that I somehow pushed further and further out. It was always a short-term issue: just one more year, just one more search ending in a hire, just 5% more profit, just after this next critical employee transition. Of course, the rewards were coming, but just not quite when we thought. Short-term successes were not celebrated personally, although I tried to set reminders — yes, literal calendar reminders — to congratulate my team and keep everyone "jazzed up" without bothering to consider how those efforts might have felt a little more genuine if I was spending time celebrating them myself. I had caught myself up in a wave of more, of setting strategic benchmarks for the organization without bothering to acknowledge a single milestone, other than to notice that when a milestone was hit, it felt "easier" than I had anticipated. In a more pure, idyllic world, these wins would have been celebrated for the end result. Instead, in my very real, very stressed, very "more" world, the only meaning derived when any milestone was achieved was that it actually wasn't as hard to hit as I thought, that all future milestones could be achieved more quickly, and that, really, I was probably doing myself a disservice by not having higher expectations of myself! The milestones grew — in length, in number, in frequency. Milestones began to be dots along a map — so that the next milestone, from its inception, was just a blip on an autobahn of hundreds of milestones that, if drawn out, would have wrapped around the globe until the entire sphere was paved over. No end in sight, no reprieve, no celebrations—just pavement, my two burning feet, and a lingering cloud of rubber and disappointed friends, family members, and ex-employees in my wake.

We returned home from Germany—by the skin of our teeth, and with a 24-hour travel day that stretched to 40+ hours after missing a connection at JFK. Our office moved to "Pandemic Fridays," meaning that everyone could use their regular working hours to run errands when stores would be less crowded or just to take some extra space and time. We launched research projects that could improve the industry. I started a non-profit called Nanny Relief Fund with a few nannies and agency owners to provide financial support for the countless nannies who lost their jobs with no notice at the onset of the pandemic. We applied for, and received, a PPP loan. In the weeks that followed, the environment shifted dramatically at Adventure Nannies as families realized (some earlier than others) that there would not be a typical school year in the fall. They would need to hire private educators—something our agency had been offering for the past five years: a revenue stream that had previously been less than 5% became over a third of our revenue in 2020.

Today, on paper, Adventure Nannies has flourished through the last two years. Our revenue and team have grown dramatically and shown no signs of slowing down. While, similar to my music career, financial success has never been an end goal, but I am incredibly grateful for building a team of amazing women who are transitioning into running the day-to-day operations.

Our team is equally passionate about helping families across the country find the support they need to pursue their dreams in a full-fledged, holistic manner, and helping nannies find professional jobs where they will be treated like the respected professionals they are. The growth has also allowed us to dedicate more time and resources to support other pieces of the domestic staffing world: the inequities in postpartum care and the birthing industry, the rights of domestic workers, and our role in being an advocate for the people who are not empowered to speak for themselves. And the small aggressions and irritants that still pop up on a daily level within my industry: another female business owner explaining how someone who doesn't have their own children could never really run a nanny agency? Sure. Thank you so much.

A mom in Park Slope believing, truly, in her heart of hearts, that the person who comes to her house to spend 60 hours a week caring for her children doesn't deserve to be paid more than the person bagging groceries at a supermarket? All right, that's an interesting perspective! A very gregarious founder explaining why going on a vacation with his family will actually be so much fun for a nanny because he and his wife are SO FUN that actually the nanny should probably pay THEM for how much fun the trip will be?! Uh huh. That's a new take. These moments used to grind at me, used to get under my skin, used to increase the volume of clacking on my laptop keyboard to the point that my dogs came over with concern in their eyes as if I was playing a drum kit at top volume.

These perceived inequities, these thoughtless, uneducated, inflexible comments, don't bother me anymore. I almost accidentally moved to Europe at the beginning of a pandemic. I cried until it felt like every ounce of liquid had been drained out of my body through my eye ducts. I sometimes have nightmares about the literal mountain of empty wine bottles my household recycled in 2020. There are a finite number of things to give power to and devote energy to at any given time, and I'm frankly relieved that my number is getting smaller, not larger. I'm alive, I always have food to eat, and I've gotten to kiss a lot of very cute people in my life. For these reasons, and many more, I consider myself lucky and now operate from a space of luck, gratitude, and relief.

It feels callous and insensitive to call anything that has occurred since March of 2020 a "silver lining." COVID-19 has destroyed the lives of millions of people, wreaked havoc on many already stressed and devalued workforces, and has caused financial ruin and dissolution of lifelong dreams and goals for so many entrepreneurs, artists, and families. Therefore, calling my story a "success story" does not fit and feels unmerited and unearned.

However, I am grateful we survived. I am thankful for the resilience, patience, and solitude the pandemic has taught me. I am grateful for my team, many of whom feel like family, or musketeers, or people who have experienced and persevered through a significant trauma together. Over the pandemic, our remote team has bought used cars from each other, shared experimental recipes, gone on camping trips together, and adopted each other's found and fostered dogs and cats. I feel connected to this particular group of staff for life. Which makes sense — we've experienced a trauma together.

While I am not sure what comes next, I do believe that the struggles each of us have endured up to this point have left us temporarily battered but stronger and more prepared for whatever lies ahead. None of us, I believe, felt confident that we would be capable of weathering ten percent of what the last two years has put us through. Yet, we are still here. And that, for today, has to be enough of a milestone for us to accept and appreciate.

About the Author

Shenandoah Davis is the co-founder and CEO of Adventure Nannies, a nationwide private staffing firm that has helped thousands of progressive families across the country find out-of-the-box nannies, private educators, and newborn care specialists.

Adventure Nannies has been featured in the New York Times, CNN, and Marie Claire. She is committed to advancing the careers and dreams of women through the realm of equitable domestic staffing throughout the United States.

In a former life, she was a singer-songwriter who was lauded by Pitchfork of creating "pitch-perfect pop" and has played over 500 shows in four continents with an intentional focus on listening rooms and all-ages spaces. Shenandoah lives in Tacoma, Washington with her partner, pups Pawlina and Batman, and rabbit, Meatball.

Connect with Shenandoah:

www.AdventureNannies.com

shenandoah@adventurenannies.com

Instagram: @adventurenannies

CHAPTER 4

The Paradox of Expectations

By Brittany Schmid

SOMETIMES, EVEN THE MOST focused and diligent of leaders tends to dig ourselves into deep, unexpected trenches, and then try to lead our own way out without quite knowing how we got there in the first place. Leadership is full of those types of paradoxes, and my story is just one example.

In 2008, I had an experience that seemingly had absolutely NOTHING to do with being a leader and seemingly EVERY-THING to do with being a woman. And yet, this paradoxical event — it was SO simple, nothing more than a phone call in the normal patterns of life, really — has transformed, informed, and improved my leadership since. Continually.

I'll bet you can relate to it in some way. As you read my story, I hope you'll begin to see where paradox — a statement that appears at first to be contradictory, but upon reflection makes sense — may be affecting your own leadership.

Today I'm the President and CEO of Dale Carnegie training in five locations throughout California, including San Diego, Los Angeles, and the Bay Area.

Back then, though, in 2008, I was in med device sales, and my territory was a pretty large region of southern California. I left home in the dark, at 4 am every day.

I was also mom to my daughter Cassidy, a toddler, and new arrival Calli, and trying to manage all the details that come with two young kids. Working, exhaustion, childcare? We figure it out. I've always been somebody who's scrappy. Go, go, go, fill every little margin! My life was like a game of Tetris constantly playing in my head, always juggling and fitting all the pieces together.

Unlike so many working moms who don't, I had great support. Kathy, my husband Brian's mom, was an excited grandparent eager to take care of the girls, and my mom would often be at my house at 4 am to fill in until Brian got home from his job as a firefighter with a non-traditional schedule.

It was all working. Until one day it didn't.

The Definition of an Upset

The phone call that shifted my outlook so abruptly was a simple one. I called my parents to ask them to babysit.

I don't remember the details but I think Brian and I wanted to go somewhere, and, of course, it was up to me to get the sitter. Like many young parents, we fell into the unspoken expectation that sitter acquisition is the mom's role.

So, I called my parents. And they said no. I remember being grateful that it was a phone call that ended quickly and not a face-to-face because I was angry and hurt that they refused.

Well, I called back and said something along the lines of, "You know, Brian's mom Kathy is always asking to watch the girls. I feel like you guys don't want to have time with them or if you do, it's only for a couple of hours at a time. I guess I just expected that my parents would want to be a part of their grand-kids' lives." I was probably being a little manipulative. Not intentionally, but probably was.

My dad immediately said, "Hold on, Brittany." (He says my name like *Britt-a-nee* when he's being his version of parental.) At the time, I heard all of my growing-up teenage snark in my head about how my dad gets when his feathers are ruffled, with this certain tone of voice and cadence to his words. I was mad and disappointed, and he knew it.

"Britt-a-nee," he said again. "Do you know what the defi-nition of an upset is?"

And I remember thinking, No, I don't, Dad, but I bet you're going to tell me.

"The definition of an upset is unmet expectations," said my dad. "We never agreed to be your babysitter. You put that expec-tation on us. We never talked about it."

I don't swear too often, but I remember thinking *freaking eff* (it makes me want to growl a little now, just thinking about it). Because he was right, damn it!

And I knew it rationally, in the moment. He WAS RIGHT. But at the same time, I was mixed with emotion because I was just wanting to serve myself and wanting my parents to serve me. Didn't they want me to have a healthy marriage and a good career and happy kids? I mean, I felt like my parents weren't feeling the same kind of reaction to their grandbabies as Brian's mom, or maybe not reacting in whatever way I thought would be normal. I put ALL of that expectation on them.

Which is silly, and I laugh about it now because, of course, they've supported me my entire life. My dad is a champion and mentor for me. But in the moment, it felt like the goodness of our relationship fell away, and they were not there for me. As I got off the phone, I realized that even though he was right and so rational and made so much sense, I also felt WRONG, like a freaking kid again, yet with kids of my own. I was pissed off, still needed a sitter, was moving on to "what's next" (as I do), and grappling with it all.

And it has stuck with me forever because my dad's lesson is still so powerful and true. And such a huge gift.

What my dad did that day — unknowingly for both of us — was introduce me to a different way of managing expectations and outcomes, which research now calls a "paradoxical mindset." For women leaders in particular who are continually faced with leadership and gender expectations that are both contradictory and complementary, embracing a paradoxical mindset can make all the difference in our leadership.

In fact, there's a 2018 study about the difference between paradoxical mindset and dilemma mindset that looks closely at the ways the "paradox mindset helps women leaders build psychological resilience, identity coexistence, and leadership effectiveness, whereas those who adopt a dilemma mindset experience depleted resilience, identity separation, and lowered leadership effectiveness."

(You can view the abstract here: https://www.sciencedirect.com/science/article/pii/S104898431 8302339)

The word "paradox" derives from the Greek word *paradoxons*, meaning contrary to expectation. My parents' decision violated my unspoken expectation and belief that if they loved their grandchildren (and me), they'd babysit.

And it continues to play out in my life and my leadership.

Unmet Expectations are Invitations to Reflect

I continue to see that lesson — the unending learning — take shape in my life when I'm upset about anything. And then I can stop and go to a higher-up balcony view and ask myself why I'm upset. *What did I expect would happen? Was that expectation clarified earlier to me or the other person? Is it appropriate that I was even expecting that of them?*

What I now know is that sometimes the most simple lessons are the most powerful, and that's how I feel about unmet expectations. We often don't recognize them as such. We don't always reflect on them the way they deserve to be reflected on. Some of us have practices of reflections about our relationships and our businesses. I believe expectations have that exact same place in our lives. They deserve to be really intentionally reflected upon and incorporated from the standpoint of communication. This is true for my relationships with my employees and clients, for my relationships with my kids and Brian, my family and friends — and most importantly — myself.

Since I bought my first Dale Carnegie franchise in 2015, I've used my interpretation of unmet expectations with near-constant awareness. It has served me in seeing when my ego is in the way, putting undeserved and unspoken expectations on others. It has served me in seeing how and when I haven't clearly communicated my expectations. It has served me in observing my employees and coaching them into seeing where and when their own unmet expectations might be creating upset or strangling outcomes.

I love the ease of it; it doesn't have to be hard. When I recognize that some expectation is being unmet, I can reexamine it at its very simplest core and ask easy questions: *I'm unhappy with what just happened. Okay, well, why? What was your expectation? Well, crap. I didn't have one. So flush that and start again.*

The lesson of "upset = unmet expectations" works, and paradoxical mindset works. It's a constant learning and reevaluation process, of course.

But it works and then one day it stopped working.

The Paradox of Expectations

Let's face it. Using the definition that a paradox is something both complementary and contradictory at the same time, I could arguably make a case that the concept of women leaders is in itself a paradox. I won't, but I could.

What I will say is that we all experience the paradox of expectations in business simply because we are women. We walk into our offices — wherever they are these days — carrying with us some assumptions that we simply do not necessarily expect from male leaders. Women in leadership are asked to be exacting yet nurturing. Commanding yet collaborative. In control yet supportive. Distant yet available. Confident yet obliging. The list goes on. And we figure it out. And we will continue to do so because we are leaders and that's what we do.

I, like almost all of us, was going about my business, reflecting, learning, earning, managing, leading and feeling pretty good about it all. I clearly understood — and still lived by the adage my dad taught me when he said, "Britt-a-nee, the definition of an upset is unmet expectations."

But what do you do when EVERYTHING changes? When expectations become moot, because in the space of what feels like a moment, the whole world changes? When the pandemic hit, it dug a leadership trench none of us expected. How do we lead ourselves out of that?

That whole "upset = unmet expectations" equation blew up for me. How could I make any kind of realistic expectation about the unknowable? The simplicity of my system disappeared. The questions: "I'm unhappy with what just happened. Okay, well why? What was your expectation?" became unanswerable. All expectations were off the table.

COVID-19 forced me to create a new relationship with my expectations, a reevaluation of the paradoxical mindset I had developed, and a completely new experience of myself as a leader.

I'd always been sort of stuck in what I'll call "imposter syndrome" for lack of a better term — something I think many leaders share. I over-analyzed every conversation. *What could I have said differently? Was I authentic enough? What did I really bring to the table? Was I even enough to be at the table?* How many ways could I beat myself up? I was my own most relentless judge — constantly thinking, criticizing, rethinking, solving.

When COVID-19 first hit, I remember one of my employees said, "I don't know if we should run the public program tomorrow." And I was like, "Wait, what?" Then as COVID-19 continued to hit, we kind of just stopped. For two weeks, we stopped our public programs, and I tried to figure out what kind of maneuvering I could do. Within the first week, I knew I didn't have the financial resources to keep the team if we weren't bringing in that money. I was moving fast, though, actually quicker than most at responding.

I remember having papers out that represented each person on the team. And I was like, *Who do I need to exit first? And how do we need to do this?* It was bizarre. And at first, like most of us, I went into it thinking it'll last two weeks. Then it'll last two months, it'll last six months. And then it kind of got to the point where a 90-day goal was a success. Then it was like, screw it. Meeting a freaking 30-day-goal is a success. All the core fundamental things imploded.

At one point, I thought I was going have to claim bankruptcy (thankfully, that did not happen) and needed to at least mentally face that. Allowing myself to go there, because I hid from it for a long time, was the most freeing experience. But at the same time — another paradox — I realized I was broken. I was very, very depressed about my business and the changes that were happening with the team.

In the disoriented environment of everything going on, I lost my sense of self. I'm grateful that one of the Dale Carnegie stress and worry principles that applies to me is, "think about the worst that can happen and then basically build from that."

So, I did.

I began to work with an executive coach who focuses on neuroscience. He gave me some tools not only to reflect and build on my own expectations of myself, but to completely rearrange how I interact with the way I think of expectations. It's a long story that I'll make short here, but, basically, we went through an emotional and deep process that refined three "pillars" that I now use to cut through the muck of my own expectations and imposter stuff. (I'll share more about it in an upcoming book about expectations, due out in late 2022.)

Those pillars: I'm grounded, I'm considerate, and I'm an activator. I now have the intention to go into every interaction knowing that if I'm grounded, I'm considerate, and I've activated, I have met my expectations. I've also honored my values and can move on and don't have to think about it again.

I initially told my coach that I wasn't able to let myself be joyful, to laugh with reckless abandon, to experience what I thought the fullness of life "should" be (unmet expectations). Now, I don't know that I'm allowing myself to be fully joyful, but I am finding, in some really cool ways, contentment and peace.

As I said, I used to be constantly thinking. I mean, disruptively! I was great at making up scenarios: *Well, what if this happened? And then, okay, well what if this pathway happened?* It was like a choose your own adventure book.

In my brain, at all times, for every freaking situation, I would have three different doors that could be selected and I'd know what would happen four chapters deep. And I used to think it was a strength and a virtue. And then of course with COVID-19, I realized I don't even want to know what other doors there are. The strength of this is it has really cleared my head, and has also opened the opportunity to be more present, which then would have the offset value of allowing me to have joy, and laugh with a little bit more reckless abandon.

I'm not looking back and being okay with it. So, as I take all of those different pieces from the original "aha" moment in 2008 to where I am now, I'm starting 2022 knowing the paradox of expectations are just part of life and I don't use "upset" to value them.

I realize I've let go of my expectations of others, or I let them know when I have them. I don't get bothered by my kids if they don't do something I never told them I expected them to do. When I feel frustration with an employee, I realize I didn't let them know my expectation or I didn't know myself. I'm also noticing when people have an expectation of me and can say,

"You seem upset," and do some work to see if there's something unmet there.

The more I interact in life, in business, in leadership, I see that it's the little things, the simple things, that often make the most impact. Being aware of and mining the gold in unmet expectations, in the paradoxes that seem so simple yet complicate our lives, certainly won't settle the world's problems by any means.

Many of us at some point in our leadership have taken on the belief that expecting other people to behave in the way we expect them to will actually make them behave that way.

My ongoing lesson about the paradox of expectations is that there's freedom in letting go, in embracing gratitude and being present in what's actually unfolding in front of me, rather than trying to control that unfolding. I urge you to reflect on yours. If we can start to recognize and communicate our expectations with each other — as leaders — it could resolve a lot and open us up to the wisdom of the paradox and the value of fostering a collective paradoxical mindset.

About the Author

Brittany Schmid is the President and CEO of Dale Carnegie training in five locations throughout California, including San Diego, Los Angeles, and the Bay Area. Her vision is elevating human potential and creating opportunities for people to do meaningful work. She lives in San Diego with her husband Brian and daughters Cassidy and Calli.

Connect with Brittany:

LinkedIn: brittany-schmid-46b2a89
brittany.schmid@dalecarnegie.com

CHAPTER 5

My Secret?
Just SHOW UP

By Daisy Jing

TODAY I'M WRITING THIS from my house in Orange County. My partner is upstairs with his many monitors in a meeting, our nanny is with our daughter downstairs. Our labradoodle is on my lap. An ocean breeze flutters in through the windows, flickering out my diptyque Baies candle. It's January 15th, 2022, and I look out my window. I see clear blue skies, hear bicycle bells, the sunshine kisses the side of my face. Am I in paradise? Well not quite, as I'm working on end-of-year taxes and reconciliation of payroll. I have about 20 minutes to finish up before I change into my lululemons and go teach my Lagree pilates class. After that, I'll need to put my daughter to bed and then work on our newest product launch — a sunscreen that I'm obsessed with and use every day.

So how at 32-years-old did I achieve this life? I didn't have a trust fund, I didn't have a rich dad or rich husband helping me along the way, I didn't have the "right" connections. My secret?

I simply showed up.

That is my biggest secret to success. Just showing up.

Showing Up #1: The Start of My Business

I was working in corporate America when I had this idea for a beauty startup, a "Yelp for Beauty Products." Never did I think in a million years would I quit my high-paying prestigious job to start a business. However, through my time struggling with acne, it was so hard for me to find good beauty products that worked for my skin type — a gal who has every skin condition under the sun, what should I use? I always wanted to create a "Yelp for Beauty Products" and I had drawn different mockups on the backs of scratch paper and stuff... but it couldn't be an actual thing, could it? I mean what would I, a 21-year-old, know about how to start a mobile app?

Later that week, I received an email from my Alumni Entrepreneurship Group: "Pitch your startup to top VCs!" it said. I had to submit a pitch deck and a video about my startup for an opportunity to get a meeting. Was this a sign? I tried to ignore it but I couldn't stop thinking about it. I mean, I had no "startup." I just had a vision. But the more I tried to ignore it, the more it bothered me. So, the night right before the pitch deadline, I tried my best to use Photoshop and create a few mockups. I started on my PowerPoint. I think it looked awful and I almost didn't submit it. I was in tears because of how horrible I felt the pitch looked. However, for whatever reason, my 10-year-old brother came in and told me not to cry and to submit it. I believed a 10-year-old's opinion. I truly believe if he hadn't come in and encouraged me, I wouldn't be where I am today. This also comes from the fact that I believe women are too hard on ourselves. If I couldn't get it perfect, I didn't want to even try. And that's where just showing up changed my life.

So, I submitted the pitch. I forgot about it, and a month later, I received an email saying my business (which wasn't really a business, remember, it was just a PowerPoint) was selected out of 50+ pitches to present to investors in New York City. My mouth dropped open. *WHAT? How was I going to do this?*

Even before I could talk myself out of it — how I wasn't "ready enough" and it was a fluke they chose me to pitch this pretend business — I booked a nonrefundable plane ticket to NYC so I would have to pitch.

The next couple of months before the pitch, I worked my ass off night and day to get this "fake business" off the ground. I had extreme anxiety every night because I felt like a fraud. I remember right before my pitch, I was a nervous wreck. My knees were shaking, I was sweating through my tweed pencil dress. I gave my best four-minute pitch. I was so nervous during the Q&A, thinking, *would these venture capitalists know that I hadn't even launched my startup yet?* I tried to remember all the research papers I had read and studied. Oh, and one venture capitalist asked, "You know, I'm not sure about beauty products, well, I mean, I've never used them, I'll have to ask my wife, but do beauty products actually perform differently on different women?" That was his question. That was it.

Even though I didn't win the pitch competition, I was so proud of myself. I took a dream I had in my head and shared my vision in front of top venture capitalists. It was at that moment I felt like I could do anything.

It was only because I showed up.

Showing UP: To EO

EO, or Entrepreneur's Organization, has been a huge asset to me personally. When I started Banish, I had no idea what I was doing. There's an analogy of entrepreneurship: it's like jumping off a plane and building a parachute on the way down. That's how I felt when starting my business.

For the first few years of my business, I felt incredibly lonely and isolated. There were so many issues and problems I faced, and I didn't have the support structure. I had to Google everything, I felt like I was skydiving without a parachute and at any moment, I'd pull the cord and the parachute wouldn't be there.

Funny thing though, I actually found out about EO from the book *Million Dollar Women* by Julia Pimsleur. I remember her talking about it in her book. I didn't think too much of it until

I was in an Uber ride and had met another entrepreneur who thought about joining EO. Then, just out of the blue, one Saturday night I applied. It didn't take too long, probably less than 15 minutes.

I got an email a month later asking me to go to a "Prospective New Member" networking event. I remember it was in a Nespresso® store in Beverly Hills. Sure, why not? There was a fitness studio I loved right in Beverly Hills so I signed up for a class right beforehand. I'd pop right in!

Walking to the networking event, I was a bit sweaty, but I thought my black sweatshirt would cover up any sweat marks from my tank. When I arrived at the Nespresso® store, I thought, *Holy shit. This is not just a coffee store. This is a masterpiece.* Then I peeked in and saw everyone was an older, white male. They were all dressed in suits. I rechecked the event info in my phone, did I have the right place? Sure, it was the right date and time. I was so intimidated. I was the only woman there, the only woman under thirty there, not to mention the only woman of color — and I was wearing sweats when everyone else was wearing a suit.

But that's when I had to muster the strength and just "show up." I forced myself, even though every single muscle in my body told me not to. I entered, signed in, put my name badge on, and tried my best to try not looking awkward.

Long story short, the 1-2 hours I was there was very awkward in the beginning, but towards the end, I was able to have conversations with some prospective members. I ended up joining EO.

Through EO, I've met so many wonderful people, I have so many amazing friends, and my forum is the best! I'm contributing to this book because of EO. If I hadn't "shown up" to that Nespresso® cafe in my sweaty sweats, I wouldn't be writing this chapter today.

Showing up: Teaching Lagree

I've always been a fitness fanatic. Sometimes a fitness class is the only time in my day when I'm not on my phone or in front of my computer. Ever since the COVID-19 pandemic started, I would feel so burnt out at the end of the day with so many Zoom calls back-to-back. My favorite time of day would be the 45 minutes of my workout class. The combination of energizing music and workout high would always get my day started on a positive beat.

So, when I saw on Instagram that a Lagree studio was offering certifications, I thought about signing up for it… but then negative voices tried to talk me out of it. *Daisy, do you really have enough time to teach fitness classes? Daisy, your time is worth so much more. Daisy, you already have a business and are a new mom. Are you being selfish for doing this?*

Regardless, I just showed up to the training. I loved learning about fitness and Lagree. I loved learning about the logistics of a fitness studio. They mentioned to reach out if we were interested in auditioning to teach.

I decided to reach out for an audition. There were negative voices in my head, voices saying, Why are you qualified to teach fitness? Have you spent years teaching fitness? How do you know what you're doing? Are you fit enough to teach fitness? You should lose that muffin top, what about that back fat? Knowing that I tend to go into a negative spiral, before I could talk myself out of it, I reached out to the coach and scheduled an audition before I could even think it through.

I made it! I started teaching Saturday mornings. For me, Saturday mornings are the highlight of my week, when I'm able to finally get off my phone and have a few hours to be completely present off my computer. For those few hours on Saturday mornings, I'm completely immersed in motivating Lagree clients to push themselves and become their best selves. I love speaking, I love choosing bomb music, I love dancing, I love having fun! I'm so glad I pushed myself to "show up" outside my comfort zone.

So, ladies, if I can give one word of wisdom to you, it's simply to show up. Go out there and go outside your comfort zone. Push yourself over the edge to talk to that one person, do that one thing, ask that one question, give that one presentation, sign up for that conference, whatever it may be. Because you never know where life will lead you unless you just SHOW UP.

About the Author

Daisy Jing is founder of Banish.com, a natural skincare line targeted in treating acne scars. She suffered with acne all her life. Traditionally prescribed acne treatments didn't work for her. She studied premed/ dermatology at Duke University, and while there, Daisy started her YouTube channel reviewing skincare products. Through her vulnerability and story about sharing her skin, her YouTube channel garnered over 70M views. She started formulating her own products to help her skin, and before long, her audience wanted to buy whatever it was she was using herself. Banish was born!

Today, Banish is a multimillion-dollar business and its products are sold all over the world. Daisy is a TEDx Speaker, Inc. 500 entrepreneur, Forbes 30 Under 30, and mom to Indie Mei, her daughter, and Lily Mae, labradoodle. In her free time, Daisy loves fitness and teaches Lagree Pilates.

Connect with Daisy:

Instagram: @daiserz89
TikTok: @daiserz89
https://banish.com/
TED Talk:
https://www.ted.com/talks/daisy_jing_a_tragedy_called_perfection

CHAPTER 6

You are ONLY? WTF?

By Dr Kristin L Kahle

LET ME INTRODUCE MYSELF TO YOU. I am Dr. Kristin L. Kahle and you can call me Dr. K. If you know me, you won't be surprised that I have included WTF in the title of this article. If you don't know me, you'll get it by the end of this chapter. Either way, it means exactly what you think it means, AND it means something totally different, too, but you'll have to read to the end to find out.

A bit about me: I live in beautiful, sunny San Diego, California with my husband Hector and my two puppies (all dogs are puppies to me) — Ellie and A.J. I am an avid traveler, dedicated reader, and life-long learner.

I like to call myself the Executioner because I get shit done. I love to get a project or a task and crush it. Get it accomplished. On to the next!

I love to be the Executioner for other women in their businesses as well. It's a passion of mine — to come into a woman-owned business to design and develop automation and system integrations that jump their business to the next level.

Let's Talk a Bit of Business

I've been in the leadership trenches, if you will, for quite a while. I have successfully started, run, and sold three different companies in my life: one in my 20s, one in my 30s, and one in my 40s (and that is all I am willing to say about age). All three businesses came with great experiences, failures, successes, and learning opportunities.

My last company, NavigateHCR, was a unique one that brought with it some significant lessons.

When the Affordable Care Act (ACA) passed during the Obama administration, I was in the beginning stages of my Doctorate degree. Well, I am an insurance professional so one weekend I decided to read that bill, and by the way, I am sure I read it long before anyone in our government read it.

At the time, the ACA was over 3000 pages, so I snuggled in with it on a long San Diego weekend. When I finished it, I thought, Oh shit! No one knows what is in this and no one knows what is going to happen to the employers impacted by it!

I decided then and there that I was going to write my dissertation on this topic and start a company to support businesses that had no idea what was about to be thrown at them.

For the next four years, I did research, lobby work, speaking engagements, wrote papers, and wrote my dissertation all around this topic. I was so immersed in it I got to the point that when I sat down on an airplane and someone asked me what I did for a living, I told them I was a cocktail waitress. I mean, I had spoken about this bill for four straight years at this point. What was I going to say? I talk every day about the IRS, how sexy is that?

I made it my job and my vision to protect American businesses from what was coming from this legislation. When you think about why people go into business, it is not to fill out paperwork for the government. They are there to offer some product or solution that they are passionate about, and the ACA was and is just another pain in the ass that they have to accomplish to meet a deadline.

However, this bill was highly politicized and came with anger and backlash from business owners. Fortunately, I have thick skin and I'm so great at providing solutions that I could avoid the political conversation. I would say, "Hey, just let me help you and I can get you out of all the fines and fees, but we have to talk about all the other items that go with it." As I said, at this point I'd been talking about this topic 80-120 days a year, every year, for four years straight.

While I was doing that, I was also working as a consultant for a firm that was considering developing a game plan around Employer Assistance for this bill. I decided to stop doing that and start my own company to develop a service-based product that could help businesses with the data and filing, and provide an expert (me) who could answer their gazillions of questions about the ACA. At this point, no one had done this before. It was like the blind leading the blind.

The ACA War Room

So, I studied — I'm good at that, too — and began to figure out what needed to happen. If you have ever spent any time on tax formulas, you will know that this was and is a very complicated formula. It was not 2+2=4. It was more like, if X happens and then Y happens and maybe they throw in a Z, then it spits out a code. But the Xs and Ys and Zs were always changing, and the codes were confusing, and really, WTF?

I formed a war room in my office: white boards, sticky notes, different-colored pens, and everything else I could buy at an office supply store. I really got into the formulas. With all my speaking opportunities, I had established about 40 clients. I had no idea what to charge them and had no idea what I was going to deliver. All I knew was that I was going to help them with this problem.

My war room was littered with diet soda and snacks and Post-it® Notes and I knew that I would figure this out. My dad once said that one of my greatest strengths is that I can take a complicated subject and make it easy to understand, so I focused on dissecting and simplifying.

It took me some time, but I finally figured out the formula. I'm the Executioner, so okay, clients, let's go, let's get this done! I am here to help! I started in on the process of creating the necessary forms and timelines for the deliverables.

And just like that, the IRS moved the deadline out a year. ONE YEAR!

Part of me was excited and overjoyed about that, but another part of me was like, Now what? What do I do for a year? How can I control something that I have no control over? What should I say to my clients? Should I refund the money? Do I clean up the war room or buy more diet soda, snacks, and office supplies?

After a long, two-day thought process, I came up with a solution.

The ACA and Dr. K

Here is what I did. I invested more money (that I did not have) in the company. I hired a marketing firm and some staff. I worked in the evenings doing various jobs and sold my purses, car, jewelry, and clothes. I put that money into the company to really go after new clients and create a service offering that employers needed and wanted.

I remember one payroll period when I only had enough money in my account to cover two out of my four employees. So, I went to the bank and cashed out my credit cards to get more money and I was still short. My husband came to the rescue with his own money (he is my biggest cheerleader).

We ultimately created a service offering that no one had in the marketplace (still to this day no one else offers what we created).

So off we went into the country to sell this product to employers impacted and sell it we did! Soon we were at $1,000,000 in revenue and climbing. Office space was tight. I had multiple people in offices, people on the floors, and people in the stairwells making calls and appointments. We did move to a new space, but not before I accomplished the other huge milestone I'd been working on through all of this: passing my dissertation and finally becoming Dr. K.

The Software Shower Moment

So, success, right? We had services, staff, clients, and new office space. All was going great until one day I had one of those AHA! shower moments (don't we all have them?) when I decided that instead of a service-based business, I wanted to be a software company!

Ask me what I knew about creating and running a software company. NOTHING!

I went looking for some version of *How to Start a Software Company for Dummies* and could not find it. So back to the war room I went! In a period of two years, I made every mistake there was when it came to software. I also learned a great deal, read a ton, took a few classes, and designed a software company that was (and still is) awesome.

While I was learning about software, I noticed that every time I spoke to my women business owner friends and asked them about any new software or new automation tools that they were using, I would get a pretty blank stare.

So, I started asking them questions, "How do you assign tasks? How do you communicate? How do you build your dashboards? How are you doing your handoffs from one employee to the next?" Again, I got very blank stares. One very important lesson from this research was that my male business owners were having these discussions around software, automation, power flows and bots, but my female business owners were not.

Back to the fucking war room I go, this time to look at workflow in our software and communication workflow. I have all the control in the software to build out all the automatic processes, but how? In email? How do I communicate with onshore and offshore teams? I was ahead of the curve with multiple employees in multiple locations both on and off shore and needed ways to build a team.

I built it out, making sure that our team had the tools that they wanted and needed and the business had the visibility that I needed, and over the next two years, I created a game plan that communicated and delivered services to our clients.

We really and truly had become a software-as-a-service-technology company that could deliver seamless services via a portal. Once we had the proof of concept, it was time to consider selling. I always knew that I wanted to sell the company within five years of starting it. I decided it was time to look into that offering and hired an executive board to help me with the vetting of vendors for the sale. I won't bore you with the details but I sold the business and the process took about a year.

You Are ONLY...

When you sell your business, the first year is definitely the honeymoon phase. I was over the moon with my decision, and, of course, stayed on to consult with the company that purchased mine.

However, that company was not a technology company. Our business is a departure from their other core businesses and the way we worked was foreign to them. Every single meeting, I would have to explain what it is that we do, re-explain the software, make the case for why we did things the way we did them, and eventually and finally came the time to meet with and dive deep into their software team.

For that, of course, I wanted to do what I do so well — take our difficult services, our new-to-them technology — and present it in a way that makes it easy for everyone to understand. Walking into that meeting, I had on a kick-ass dress, my hair, makeup, and jewelry were styling, and I was ready to go.

I started my presentation and all was going well until one comment was made… the comment was, "But you are ONLY a salesperson." And it was said by someone who'd been along for the entire transition.

I'm not going to lie, it threw me.

Um, I'm WHAT? I am what? Are you fucking kidding me? Did you not hear my journey and all the learning and courses and thought process I have around technology? I BUILT that company. In my mind, I was yelling and screaming, I am not ONLY anything!

Of course, as all of us have been at times (especially women), I was put in the bucket that person wanted to put me in. I went down the rabbit hole a little bit (not too far) feeling like I had no value to the company that bought my company, that if I'm

YOU ARE ONLY? WTF?

not selling, I have no worth, etc. And of course, I know none of that is true.

WTF

This is far from the first time I've had an experience like this. Many of them are included in my book, *NOtivation. Use the Power of NO to Make Your First Million Dollars.*

I am motivated by being told "no," and this felt a little like that. Making the decision to move forward from that comment — that I am ONLY something — was a little challenging for me. I think it stung so much because it came from someone I respected and I doubt that he is even aware of how much his words affected me.

However, there's beauty in it because it sent me back to the war room to design another company. I love that fucking war room with its walls painted in white chalkboard paint! My decision to build another company was NOtivated to make sure that no other woman gets put in that position — that feeling of being told she's ONLY something — and make sure she's armed with the tools and automation that she needs to run her successful business.

Moving forward, my passion is to help women. So, the next time I ask questions to women entrepreneurs like I asked when I was doing my research, I don't get blank stares. My goal is that women business owners are also discussing software, automation, power flows and bots.

My next services, software, and solutions (the big three) company will help women entrepreneurs understand the ways technology can free up their time and give them the visibility they need to grow.

Guess what I'm calling it? Women Technologies Foundation, or WTF. I can't wait to see what happens, and I know it won't be ONLY one thing!

About the Author

Being the CEO and Founder of a successful company, author of two books, business coach, consultant AND athlete is the way Dr. Kristin L. Kahle proves that women are NOT the "weak sex", but quite the opposite.

NavigateHCR is the name of the company that Dr. K (the way we are going to call Kristin Kahle from now on because it sounds like a bad-ass rapper) leads right now. She managed to search for a solid team conformed of talented specialists who assist brokers, employers, team leaders, and other companies on everything related to HR compliance, healthcare law, ACA, and many more legislative developments.

Dr. K has found a way to use technology and make all these confusing (yet important) processes easier. And as if that wasn't enough, she also LOVES sharing her knowledge! That's why she dedicates some of her free time to coaching business owners. Especially the ones owned by women.

Dr. K is also kind of nerdy. She is a Certified Healthcare Reform Specialist, owns a DBA from Argosy University, an MBA from the University of Phoenix, and a BA from Pine Manor College. Besides that, she has two published books where she describes the two steps of building a business: failing and standing up again, so as saying "no" when it's needed in order to become successful.

The first step is developed in "Crash and Learn", where Dr. K and many other well-named entrepreneurs tell their stories on failing and how to move on from that situation. Then in "Notivation" she uses the most powerful tool (sense of humor) to explain how saying "No" will lead business owners to better decisions. Plus, Dr. K structured the book thinking on how to help entrepreneurs to win their first million dollars!

Now you know. A mentor doesn't always have to look like Obi-Wan or Dumbledore. Your mentor can be fun, creative, empathic, a lover of music and sports, and with wild hair. Just as Dr. K is!

Connect with Dr. Kahle:

https://www.LinkedIn.com/in/drkristinkahle/
https://www.Facebook.com/drkkahle
https://drkristinkahle.com/

CHAPTER 7

Miracles are Ours

By Hazel Ortega

YOU MAY BE WONDERING WHO I am to be talking about miracles. That's exactly what I would be thinking if I was sitting in your place. But, in fact, that is how my miracle making began! It took a miracle for me to see beyond my sob story.

I grew up in downtown Los Angeles in an 800-square-foot apartment in a five-kid, one-parent household. My family was on welfare. The kids in my neighborhood were routinely involved in drugs and gangs. Teen pregnancy was a huge issue. Drive-by shootings were commonplace. My own cousin was killed in one of those shootings.

Me in 9th grade, posing with the neighborhood gang's graffiti

The first miracle of my life came on a day when I was sitting on the curb outside my mom's apartment. I was holding a plastic laundry basket containing the few possessions I was able to grab on my way out the door. I was 19-years-old and my mom had kicked me out of the apartment after a confrontation.

My two younger sisters had been accepted into an upward bound program at Occidental College. After several warnings, they were told if they missed another session they would be thrown out of the program. They were devastated. Even though the program in Eagle Rock was only seven miles away from our apartment, it may as well have been in another country. My mom came up with every excuse not to drive them there: she was too busy, she was hung over, there was no gas in the car. She didn't value or understand the opportunity this program offered my sisters, but I did.

My mother was in bed, refusing to get up and even take my sisters to the nearby bus stop so they could get to the college. My sisters were frantically begging her to get up, but she wouldn't move. Fed up, I screamed at my mom to get out of bed and be a better mother.

My mother stunned me by springing up out of bed, grabbing me by my blouse, and yelling that I had one minute to grab as much of my stuff as I could and get out.

All I could get my hands on was a jacket, two pairs of shoes, a couple of notebooks, a photo album, my makeup bag, and a few dirty clothes before my mother pushed me out the door and onto the street. I sank down onto the curb, not sure what to do with myself.

However, because of my actions that day, my mother ended up driving my sisters to their upward bound program. They became the first members of our family to ever go to college. That is a miracle!

As for myself, I had flunked out of high school and couldn't see any future for myself at the time, but I did see a future for my sisters. I fought hard with my mom to get them to the program that day. It was almost a year before my mom spoke to me again, but it was worth it.

Several years and countless conflicts and dramas later, I attended a personal development seminar. Dozens of people were lining up to go on stage and defend their life stories, to challenge the idea that they were responsible for how their lives turned out. I sat for three days and listened to all of their stories. In the back of my mind there was a little voice saying, Yes, that's true for them. They are creating their stories, but none of these stories are worse than mine.

I had been sitting in the seminar for about four hours when I heard a story that stopped that voice in my head. A young woman, about 27-years-old, confidently walked up to the microphone. She began to talk about how her older sisters did not love her. They did not call her, ask about her, or look for her when she didn't come around. When she was a kid, they would slam their bedroom doors in her face.

Then she moved on with her story. She had a different father than her sisters. When she was just a toddler, her father molested her 13-year-old stepsister and got her pregnant. Even when her mother found out about it, she did not leave him.

Soon after that, at a family party, she was playing with her father, sitting in his lap when one of her cousins, enraged about the molestation, shot and killed him. She said his blood was all over her. She was only three-years-old when it happened. As she told the story, she was extremely emotional, sobbing. She went into great detail about it. I felt as if I was standing right there in that living room with her.

It was a horrendous, shocking story. I thought that was the worst thing that could ever happen, your father being killed right in front of you when you're a child. It was so sad. It made me think that compared to hers, my story was nothing.

In that moment, the myth that my story was different and worse was completely busted. I had thought that I had this untouchable story and so many reasons for people to feel sorry for me. That day I saw an opening where I could change things for myself. Up until then, I had been using my story as proof of why my life wasn't working. I had already been making some changes in my life, but my story had a strong hold on me. Against the odds, I had just completed a hard-earned Master's degree and was just starting my work as a psychologist. Despite my education and becoming a professional, there was still all of the old drama and pain inside of me from my upbringing.

After I heard this young woman's story at the conference, I clearly understood how we create and add so much bullshit to the stories of our lives. We contribute so much unsubstantiated detail without any proof. We just allow our insecurities and suspicious minds to run amok.

Another example of creating or worsening our problems can do with money. When I was growing up, all of my friends and family believed that money was scarce. My own mother never had a checking account. She would hide what little money she had in the walls of our apartment. She would literally poke a hole in the wall, roll up a few dollar bills and tuck them in the hole, spackle over it, then break it open when she needed the money. My friends and family all talked about money problems a lot. We made them bigger and bigger. As an adult, I remember hearing my own kids talk about how we didn't have any money because they heard me say it all the time. When I couldn't afford something they wanted, instead of saying, "Not right now," or "You have plenty of toys," I would tell them there was no money.

A big social difference I see between people with money and people without much money is the deeply-rooted belief of wealthier people that they are safe and no matter what happens, things will be fine. Even when they are hit with a large, unexpected expense, they don't despair, because they know money will come back around. They can get fired, or have their belongings stolen, but it's OK. They don't go to a place of extreme pessimism and desperation because of a setback. This attitude is actually what keeps them calm and confident. It is as if they are psychologically conditioned to be optimistic, and of course it becomes a self-fulfilling prophecy.

After I graduated from college, I started my first business in my Los Angeles garage with a business partner. We seemed like a great fit, so we launched a counseling center for injured workers as vocational counselors. We both agreed that all we wanted was to earn $4,000 each month to be able to pay our bills. The business was created on a shoestring, but eventually, it began to take off.

After a few years together, I hired a business coach who taught me about planning and creating a vision for where I want the business to go. In creating a vision for the business, I saw a totally new future and these visions became reality. I was thrilled with the process and progress, so it became my practice to create visions for everything: my "big hairy audacious" vision, five-year vision, three-year vision, one year vision, quarterly vision, monthly vision, weekly vision, and daily vision. This is how I realized I wanted to be the number one counseling center in the state of California.

Two additional locations were opened rather quickly, one in Santa Barbara and the other in San Diego County. We immediately became very busy and the business began to grow even more. But my partner wasn't happy. The growth overwhelmed her. She preferred the small business model with just one location. I told her about my plans to be number one in California and have 26 offices. This was too much for her. She became irate and told me I could keep all of the new offices and we would separate as partners. Our visions were not in sync and we could not move forward together.

Once we made this decision and I was moving full speed ahead on my own, my business grew by leaps and bounds, and I began to help more people and make more money than I had ever dared to dream about.

Things were looking up overall and I was flying high. My kids were thriving. I was traveling and I had just bought a new car. My kids were all driving and had cars. Life was going amazingly well.

Then I came home after work one day and walked out to grab the mail. Sitting in my mailbox were two letters. One from my mother and one from my father; both were written from jail.

It was such a contrast to the life I had built for myself and a very big reality check for me. Here I was living an incredible life and no one outside of my family knew that my parents were both in jail. Would my colleagues and friends even believe me if I told them? From the outside, I looked like I had lived a charmed life. It was my dirty little secret.

It was bittersweet, I suppose. I hated thinking of them in jail, but here I was, their daughter, creating a life I loved. I got out. I easily could have ended up where they did, but I chose another path. I was making a life that was not only fulfilling basic needs but was well on its way to surpassing them.

My journey has taken me from the ghetto to the Taj Mahal, with some side trips to Mount Everest, the Eiffel Tower, and the Vatican. Considering the first two decades of my life were spent in the worst, gang-infested area in LA in a 20-block radius, that's a miracle!

Over the years, I have continued to speak up and create and receive miracles. I have spoken for injured workers at the California state capital and in Oakland, which helped to change legislation and improve the quality of people's lives.

Honestly, opening up to miracles is not that complicated, although it will challenge you. I have become a Master of Miracles. Me — a ghetto girl from the roughest part of LA. And I can show you how.

There are three stages to being a Master of Miracles:

First, you must clean yourself up! Just like the story I shared about thinking no one had a worse story than me, I see many people caught up in their inner stories so much that it is no wonder they can't see miracles for themselves.

To clean yourself up I encourage you to:

- Recognize the sob stories you are telling yourself.

- Let people in as you release shame and create community.

- Stop living Groundhog Day every day — stop running the same habits, behaviors, and beliefs on repeat.

- Look in the mirror and see the lies you are telling yourself.

- Know that everything you want is on the other side of fear!

- Look honestly at your intimate relationships and what they are telling you about yourself.

Once you have begun the work of cleaning yourself up (It is a life-long endeavor!), it is time to raise the bar. It wasn't until I could see beyond the 20 x 20 block ghetto that I could move forward in my life.

Raising the bar happens when we:

- Stop settling when we can have it all!

- Become a millionaire of time by prioritizing and creating time for whatever we want.

- Look to the future and begin to see ourselves five years from now.

- Become great for ourselves! Be the person of our own dreams first.

- Stop making things hard on ourselves.

- Get right with the source of our lives…our families.

- Make a conscious choice to raise the bar in our lives.

Once we do this, finally we can move into the third stage: Live a life expecting miracles!

- Move into a way of being where we are always creating, speaking up, standing up, and owning the Miracle Maker we are.

- As we call out the miracles we see every day, we encourage more miracles to show up. This can look a lot like gratitude.

- When life hits you hard, it's easy to give up, to close your eyes to the future — any future at all. Start to see things in a new light.

- Waking up in the morning is a miracle.

- Being able to make a phone call from LA to Kathmandu is a miracle.

- A plane weighs over 735,000 pounds — it's a miracle that we can fly and not fall out of the sky!

- Giving birth is a miracle.

- All the moving parts of your body are a miracle. Eating and digesting an apple is a miracle. A human being able to climb almost 30,000 feet to the top of Mount Everest is a miracle.

I grew up in a rough area surrounded by drug dealers, gangs, death, and crime. Still, what right did I ever have to play a bigger victim than anyone else? What I have come to realize is that there is no quit in me. I don't believe there is any quit in you either! We all can be someone who makes a difference.

You are a miracle maker and a miracle receiver. I challenge you to begin the life-long journey of cleaning yourself up, raising the bar, and living a life expecting miracles.

Today my first business, Ortega Counseling Center, is the largest counseling center for injured workers in the state of California. Instead of being run out of my garage, it is located in a building I own in Whittier, California. I also own a company called Savvy Socks with my partner and we contribute funds to our local city office, police, and firefighters. In early 2022, I am launching High Tide Global, a non-profit foundation created to change one billion lives by 2032 through education and vision. I went from living on welfare and routinely bouncing checks to abundance, private jets, and financial freedom. I grew up in constant chaos and drama, and now I live a peaceful and drama-free life, and I created both of those experiences.

You are creating your reality. If you want more money, be on the lookout for how many times you talk about not having any. If you don't want more money, keep complaining. Pay close attention to the words you use. This is not easy but be diligent and catch yourself when you are withholding kindness or assuming negative ideas. When you change your operating system, you get to live a bigger, better life. It's like turning your life from black and white into brilliant Technicolor!

About the Author

Hazel G. Ortega is a leading expert in vocational rehabilitation for injured workers. As a formerly injured worker herself, she understands the importance of providing hope, resources, and services to injured workers. She knows first-hand how education changes people's lives and keeps families together.

Ms. Ortega's great passion is helping injured workers find joy and new ways of life after an injury. After her own injury, she fought to get an education that would lead her to the life of her dreams. As a single mother, it was incredibly challenging to take classes and care for her children, but she went full speed ahead to complete her bachelor's degree.

Later, Ms. Ortega earned her master's degree in Educational Psychology and proceeded to open the Ortega Counseling Center in 2001, ensuring the delight of her clients by fighting for their rights to education. She has owned nearly one dozen businesses, including one of LA's Top Restaurants, The Nixon in Whittier, CA, and the designer sensation, Savvy Socks.

In addition to her professional successes, Ms. Ortega created the non-profit organization, Angels for Injured Workers, AIW was created to bring financial assistance and hope to families after an injury, which is often a sudden but lengthy period. Specific activities workshops, holiday experiences, and financial assistance for basic needs (food, shelter, and utilities).

In her Amazon #1 Best-Selling book, "From Bounced Checks to Private Jets," Hazel shares her journey and guides the reader through the formula she discovered to live the life of her dreams and help others do the same.

Connect with Hazel:

Phone: 562.355.1533

ortega.hazel@gmail.com

www.themasteryofmiracles.com

CHAPTER 8

When Failure is NOT an Option

By Helena Gibson

WHEN I WAS ASKED TO WRITE a chapter in this book alongside my amazing peers, I jumped on the opportunity to share some of my story. I hoped that if even just one person could learn from my experience, that would've been a win.

These days, I'm living my dream life in San Diego. I'm a serial entrepreneur who's passionate (well, maybe a little obsessed!) about entrepreneurship, lifestyle, and mindset. It's been over two decades since I was a single mom beginning my entrepreneurial adventures with a new business (an auto repair shop at 23-years-old, if you can believe it) and struggling to make ends meet. I learned the hard way about self-doubt, burnout, and made many mistakes along the way. After the auto repair venture, I opened

Strut Hair Solutions in 2003 and figured out the trifecta of what it meant to have a successful life and business. I found the way to scale, systematize, and increase revenue to create the business of my dreams.

My journey to this point has not been easy, and I don't have all the answers. But, I am committed to sharing with you one of the many obstacles I've dealt with to get to where I am now.

It was not easy to pick just one obstacle as there have been many. (You can't have been in business for 20 years and this not be the case.) This obstacle is one of perseverance, belief in yourself when no one else does, and the will to succeed no matter what — and I think this will benefit you as well.

As I have gone along this journey, the one thing I know for sure is that your beliefs and your mindset have the most impact on whether or not you succeed.

The obstacle I choose to share in this book is my journey from leaving my shop and family in Fresno, CA to moving as a single mom with my daughter, who was 12-years-old at the time, to San Diego, CA, where I had just one friend. For reference, the distance between the two cities is 320 miles, or six hours by car.

Now, let me give you a bit of background before I begin so you have some context about how this adventure started.

My now-hair-empire started on a cart in the local Fresno mall. Yes, the ones in the middle of the mall where the employees ask you if you want to try one of their wares. After dealing with mall hours (which are very long), fines (if you are not open during their hours), and the holiday rents (they would triple in November and December), I needed a "real" store. I had proven that my concept was needed and that I was capable, so it was time to take the first step in growth.

When it comes to flippant comments, I'm the type of person who plays them on repeat and they fuel me to do exactly what someone underestimates about me. I remember a cavalier comment that my mom said while I was still working at the cart, "You don't own a business; you own a job."

That struck a chord in me. At first, I wasn't sure exactly what she meant. After reflection, though, I realized that she was right, and that was the final straw when it came to working in the mall — I knew I had to open a real store. The cart was owning me and my entire schedule.

And so, a year after opening the cart, I finally moved into a strip center. The dynamics were so different from the mall, as I didn't have hundreds of potential customers walking by me each day. I had to learn how to market to drive-by clients and entice them into my physical location. I had to learn what a CRM (Customer Retention Management) system was, create a system for electric bills, put up shelves by myself, and the list goes on. Now I owned a real business... (ha ha!).

After about two and a half years as an in-line business situated between two others, it just so happened that the anchor spot for that center had just come available after being an ice cream shop for the past 25 years. I jumped at the opportunity to move into it. I really thought about it and I knew that if I wanted to blow past my competitors in this market and make a real difference in my daughter's life (I didn't want her to miss out on anything and it was all on me because it was just me supporting her), I had to figure out a way to get into this space. This would be my first game-changing decision.

This took a lot of convincing on my end with the landlords, as the space was almost double in size — and so was the rent. I showed them how my business was steadily growing and begged them to take a chance on me. I told them I knew I could do it if given the opportunity, and thank goodness they gave that to me! This was my first experience with the power of belief and mindset. The fact that I sincerely believed I could do it got through to my landlords.

Then came beauty school. I had just moved into this new location and I decided that I was never going to leave this industry. I just loved what I was doing and the impact I was making on women's lives, so I enrolled in beauty school. I was about 30-years-old at the time.

Getting me to graduation was a team effort. I'd drop my daughter off at school in the mornings and then head to class. One of my staff members would pick her up and take her to the shop, where she'd play in the back room and wait, and I'd leave class to get there right before the store closed.

Remember how I mentioned that flippant comments sit with me and bother me? (I definitely took them more seriously than

I should have.) Well, here came another. My then-boyfriend would tease me with the "Beauty School Dropout" song from Grease. This went on for two years, which was the longest the school allowed for completion, or you had to pay overtime fees. Most of the students were there full-time and got out in nine months, but I was running a business and had to stop school hours at 4:30 pm to get to the store and get my daughter before we closed. But, in the end, I did it. In spite of all the challenges, and those flippant comments which only fueled my gusto to prove them wrong, I actually did it. In fact, as I write this very paragraph, I'm not even sure how I managed.

While I was going to school, I had to learn how to run my growing business remotely since I was in class most days, all day. After returning to my store full-time after completing beauty school, I then decided that it was time to expand to a second location, because I now knew how to remotely manage my team.

In March 2010, while I only had my Fresno location, I had gone to San Diego for a friend's birthday and fell in love with the city. I was in a city called Del Mar, sitting on the balcony of the hotel where we were staying. I was staring out at the ocean, and looking at all the beautiful people coming in and out of the hotel. As I sat there, this vision came to me of a multitude of possibilities. That I could move here and create something even more for my daughter and I. Fresno is a (relatively) small town, and San Diego felt like a whole new world. I knew this was where my daughter had to go to high school; there would be so many more opportunities for her and for me. And I needed more — I had become a big fish in a small pond in Fresno, which I admit was really hard to leave behind. It was comfortable and I had a support system. It was all I had ever known.

But I had this feeling in my heart that I had done my time here. My daughter was not a baby anymore and was actively learning in 6th grade, and it was time to see what I could do in a bigger city. It was time to leave my small town behind.

Now, imagining all of this new life I had created in my mind was one thing, but making it a reality was quite another.

It took me a year to the day to make the big move. I got a lot of pushback from family and friends when I told them about my plans and what I was going to do.

I'll never forget when I told my accountant I was doing this. He gave me a long lecture that my Fresno business would drop by at least 20% and he advised against it. But I couldn't help thinking Nordstrom, Macy's… all these companies I knew (obviously) didn't have their founders sitting in their stores! They took a chance, built systems, and opened other locations. I kept reflecting on the question: "How does a business scale if the owner is always in it?" I knew that my accountant was correct about the sales drop; that does happen when the founder steps out. However, I believed I could make it up in volume. Now, in theory, I would have 100% of the San Diego store to offset the loss where I was an absentee owner (in Fresno). If these other big businesses could do it (having started out small, like mine), I was crazy enough to think, *Why can't I do it, too?*

And then my family. How you have to love them! They meant well, but my mom got so tired of me talking about moving that finally she said, "Well would you just move already then?" To her credit, my mom told me years later that she said this to help me, and that it was her way of helping me take the leap (because she knew how I'd hang on to comments like that). What's more, my grandparents assured me that if I didn't make it there in San

Diego, that they would pay for the moving truck to bring us back. I remember telling them that if I didn't make it in San Diego, I'd be moving to Arizona. Not back to Fresno!

I had to keep telling myself that I could do this, believing in that vision I saw sitting on that hotel balcony. There was every reason it wasn't going to work and no proof that it would, other than my will to succeed. Failure was not an option. I had to be an example for my daughter, to be able to say that I at least tried and went after my dreams.

I also told my daughter that I needed her to believe in me. I told her that the move could certainly bankrupt us, but that if it didn't, life as we knew it would never be the same. I had to sell her on this dream I had, too. I was ripping her away from all she'd ever known: her friends, her family, her junior high school (which she loved), and any other ties she had to her hometown. I was afraid that since she was at "that age" (the classic preteen age), she would give me a problem or not want to go. Maybe she'd ask to stay with my mom. I didn't know. I just knew there were bigger things out there for us. But, it turned out that she fully trusted me, and it was us against the world.

I had to keep my mind in-check and focus on what could be.

I mentioned that it took us a year to move. That's because it took a year before I could find someone to rent a house to us. Remember, I was leaving my business in Fresno and didn't have a business in San Diego yet. I drove down many times over that year to look at rentals and potential shop spaces that I had found on Craigslist. Every time, it was the same thing: "No."

When it came to house rentals, I took the "No" answers a little bit better. I understood where the house landlords were coming from, how would I pay the rent if I didn't have a job here, etc. But the space brokers for commercial property… they were the worst.

One space in Del Mar wanted a huge balance in my account after I opened. This was in case I couldn't make rent. One space in Encinitas said they would lease to me, but she didn't think we'd make it, so she wanted a double deposit. She actually said that to my face. I said a resounding "NO" to both. I couldn't have that negativity around me in my dream city. They were betting on me to fail; I wasn't about to have that type of energy.

HELENA GIBSON

That process took a whopping 11 months. I was starting to lose hope. How could I start a business if I didn't live there or have a space to sell my products? I was getting so discouraged, not to mention embarrassed because I had told everyone we were moving!

It was February of 2011. As the story always goes, I went to the last open house and — go figure — the owners were entrepreneurs themselves! They loved what I was doing and were willing to take a chance on me. We got the house! We moved on March 3rd, 2011! One obstacle down.

We moved in, then I continued the search to find a space for the new store. March, April, and even May passed by with no luck. I was getting discouraged again. It had been over two months and I had to tell my daughter that we weren't going to make it here if I couldn't find a space. The Fresno store didn't do enough volume to support the higher cost of living in Southern California. I didn't know how much longer I could hang on.

Mother's Day came along and I was going to meet my friend for brunch. (This was a friend whose wedding I had attended a year earlier, who inspired me to move to San Diego). I was driv-

131

ing to Solana Beach to meet her. I saw a "For Lease" sign in a window I passed, and took down the number. The next day, I called and went to see the space.

The landlord wouldn't meet with me. He told me to get ahold of two of the owners in the center and talk with them first, then we could talk. Basically, I had to sell both of those ladies on me and my plans, and they would report back to him.

I passed their approval and then met with him. He took a liking to my story about my want for a better life for myself and daughter. He took a chance on me and believed in me.

It has been ten-and-a-half years since that day. I often thank my landlord, because if it wasn't for him believing in me, this story might have taken place in Arizona!

As a funny side note, remember the center in Encinitas, where the landlord told me that she didn't think I'd make it here? Well, that space has turned over at least four times in the 10 years that I've been in Solana Beach.

I had so many reasons to give up. I was told "no" countless times, but I believed in the vision I saw for my future. My pride and ego just couldn't let me stop trying. I couldn't fail. Everybody was watching.

Our mind is such a powerful thing. It wants to protect us and likes what it knows, what's familiar. It says, You're comfortable. Why do you want to rock the boat?

The unknown is scary, but in the unknown is where, I believe, we stretch ourselves and become so much more. Sometimes, the only person who believes in you is YOU.

Even if we fail — and everyone does at some point, absolutely everyone — we are that much closer to our dream.

What is your dream? I encourage you to take the time to dream of what could be.

What do you want out of this life? We only get one go around.

Transparently, I'm still hard on myself too. I have made some amazing friends in the ten years I've been in San Diego, and I am guilty of comparing myself to them and their successes. I think of all the "shoulds." "I should have done this, I should have done that, what if I had done this?"

But what I've discovered in the last two years is that I'm running my own race. The only person I'm in competition with is the woman I was yesterday. If you get nothing else from my story, I hope this last sentence sticks with you and reminds you that you've got this.

You can schedule a call or access my free downloads at Helenagibson.com.

About the Author

Helena Gibson is a serial entrepreneur, creator of the 7-Figure Salon, founder of Strut Hair Solutions, and a single mom. She is also an educator, author, NLP master, and podcaster.

Helena's parlay into entrepreneurship began with an auto repair shop back in 2002. That's right: Manhattan Motors. Helena was just 23-years-old at the time. For her, becoming resourceful despite a lack of experience and financial resources was simply doing whatever it took.

She completely changed paths after she saw her mother struggling with hair loss. Helena watched her mom try to find solutions for her hair loss and realized that many other women were struggling with the same thing. In short, Helena saw a need, so she started Strut Hair Solutions.

Helena is still very hands-on in her businesses. Her business is her passion, and she's dedicated to making a positive impact in her community and to having each client looking and feeling their best.

Helena recently decided that she wanted to make an impact on the hair and beauty industry and share all of her industry knowledge from the twenty years she had successfully grown Strut.

Thus, Helena created the Salon MBA program with the mission to empower 1,000 salon owners by 2025 to create profitable 7-figure businesses and enable them to have an impact on their families and communities.

In all of Helena's business endeavors, she is passionate and gives 110%. Her magnetic personality has helped foster an amazing community of women we call the "Strut Tribe."

Connect with Helena:

HelenaGibson.com

helena@struthairsolutions.com

LinkedIn: helena-gibson-5a672820

CHAPTER 9

Getting Real

By Anna (Anya) Crowe

GROWING UP AS A RUSSIAN IMMIGRANT in the US — in
New York of all places — I became immensely passionate about
authenticity and understanding who I am at the core and what
unique abilities I bring to the world. My inability to speak
English or understand others turned me inward at a young age,
giving me the opportunity to self-reflect as I worked tirelessly to
communicate with others. So much so, that, years later after
mastering the language and culture (and after three years of
building my current business), I dove fully into this topic.

What started with independent research and interviews turned
into a 164-page book, which led to a podcast and speaking

engagements. I spoke to over 200 CEOs, leaders, and entrepreneurs about authenticity and what it takes to create meaningful connections. Through these conversations, there was undisputed alignment around the significance of being real. People voiced that every significant relationship came from a genuine connection — a time when they could be their true selves. Everyone found a rewarding life, a peaceful mind, and was enroute to maximizing their potential when they were being real.

And that was the premise of my first book. *Get Real: The Power of Genuine Leadership, A Transparent Culture and an Authentic You* shared my journey to authenticity and what I believed it took to be a genuine leader and build a culture of transparency. Naturally, it also spoke about building authentic brands — I am in public relations, after all.

I didn't recognize this then, but I think one of the motivators for starting this business was to create a company that helped scale companies through strategic PR and marketing tactics and centered around a culture of transparency. A company built on internal and external trust, where employees could leverage their strengths (aka superpowers) and openly give and receive feedback knowing it came from the right place. One that sets the standard for the industry.

In that book, and through the speaking engagements that ensued, I spoke passionately about authentic leadership and its magnificent impact on an organization. I identified key authenticity habits — the ability to be human and consistent, the importance of standing behind your word, remembering it's OK not to know (and being vulnerable enough to show it), and owning your mistakes. And I tried to lead by example every single day. In retrospect, I believe it was that authenticity that helped grow our business to over a million dollars in the first couple of years and build a strong team. And I think it's that authenticity that has helped me create genuine relationships throughout the years. I truly embraced authentic leadership and thought I knew all there was to know.

And that's the beauty of this concept — the ability to be real. The fact is, I can tell you now that what I knew then was barely scratching the surface. Because when the pandemic hit (and I found myself in one physical place for an extended period), I started to see flaws in my design. My own, internal authentic design. All this time that I had been embracing authentic leadership, I was missing a key ingredient that would propel me to the next level. Yes, being human, genuine, and creating authentic connections has gotten me to a beautiful place and career, but there was still so much unknown. So much to uncover in order to get to the next level, both personally and professionally. And it was the only way to get to the next level. Going deeper to get higher.

In addition to trying to keep the business afloat and attempting to home school my two elementary school-aged boys amidst governmental restrictions, lockdown and uncertainty, I doubled down on authenticity and ventured down a strangely familiar yet unrecognizable path.

To paint a clearer picture, at that time (two months into the lockdown), our hospitality division — one of three business units — had taken a substantial hit, and as with many leaders, I was tasked with rethinking strategy and holding on to staff. What became evident at this time was that I was more fearful of being stuck as a leader than the challenges I was undergoing due to the pandemic. I realized that I had started to plateau several months before and I wasn't sure why.

For the driven and the high achievers, plateauing can often appear as failure. Upon reflection, I realized that for some reason, I was standing in the way of my own success and preventing myself from getting to the next level, both personally and professionally. As Carrie Bradshaw famously penned, "I couldn't help but wonder" what I was authentically missing and what could I do, learn, or change to maximize my own potential. And who would have known that the answer was buried inside of me, obstructed from view?

My curious, problem-solving side enabled me to dive right in, and what I discovered about authenticity in the months that followed was eye opening.

There are common conditions that plague leaders that prevent us from going to the next level. For some, it's the imposter syndrome (which, by the way, impacts four out of five CEOs — high-level high achievers); for others, it's the fear of failure, insecurity, a scarcity mindset, guilt, the need to be accepted, and more. My research showed that out of 580 million entrepreneurs in the world nearly 85% doubt their abilities and feel like a fraud. That is a lot of people not living, loving, and leading from their authentic place and feeling stuck in some capacity.

There's usually a good reason for these afflictions, with a sizable amount stemming from past experiences. Perhaps you had your heart broken years ago and now there's a part of you that's afraid of getting hurt again, so a layer of protection stays with you. Or someone once told you you're not good enough so you carry that burden in the back of your mind, casting doubt on your endeavors. Or you grew up in tough conditions, which prevents you from asking for more or thinking bigger.

The impact from our journey is real and stays with most of us for years, but what I hadn't known up until this point is the actual physical implication of past experiences. In these past months, I learned there are actual biological blockers that cause our brain to act a certain way and relive past experiences without us realizing it. These neuropathways are continuously sending signals to the brain, often stopping us in our tracks. And without physically breaking those formed neuropathways that developed from years of circumstances, most leaders fall back into unhelpful patterns and doubts, regardless of our experience or awareness.

I'm not a psychologist or neuroscientist that can identify everyone's unique stressors, but what I learned in mastering my own challenges has gotten me closer to my authentic self — to the core — than I ever imagined. And that, in turn, has greatly elevated my personal and professional life, including my leadership style. Just when I thought I couldn't be more authentic, I found new ways to remove internal roadblocks and elevate my true self. And as I dove deeper and identified my own blockers and learned how to overcome them, I found myself walking taller, shining brighter, and I saw a miraculous transformation, especially when it comes to leadership and business ownership.

I know some of this may seem a little "woo-woo" and that's OK. It did to me, too. But what's wrong with a little magic if it helps you become who you truly are? Isn't that the gift of a lifetime?

As I continue to study and write on this topic, I thought I'd share some of the lessons I've learned along the way.

Consider the Past as a Gateway to the Future.

I've never been one to dwell on the past and I don't recommend analyzing what could have or should have been. The past is the past, right? Yet, there's beauty in understanding the ways certain occurrences, traumas, and people have impacted your life. In fact, knowing this can do wonders for understanding your triggers and what's preventing you from reaching the next level.

Underneath those layers is your core self — the way you were intended to be — so getting to know the extraneous parts of you can help guide you back to your authentic self. Exercises like Lifeline or the River of Life have helped me understand why I react a certain way to new situations. Having awareness around the triggers is the first step.

Stand Your Authentic Ground.

Once you have better insight into your blockers, it becomes easier to overcome doubt, guilt, insecurity, or whatever plagues you. Standing your authentic ground and shutting down parts (or voices) that keep you from reaching your potential is tough, but doable. And it can change your world. Your true self knows those thoughts aren't real and your inner core is stronger than all the layers surrounding it. Channel your authentic voice, stand your ground, fight for you — you've got this!

Express Gratitude Regularly.

Gratitude has a myriad of benefits, including certain neurological outcomes and positive emotions. When it comes to authenticity, gratitude can serve as a reminder of your unique abilities and aid in self-appreciation. An exercise that helped me through this — thanks to my executive coach and applied neuroscientist Dr. Roddy Carter — was identifying three unique abilities, aka words to describe my gifts or assets.

The first step is identifying the three powerful and positive words that best describe me. This assignment took me a few days if I'm honest. How do you narrow down your unique abilities to three key words?

Once you've identified those words, define what each one is — what does it mean to you? If one of my assets is enthusiasm, for instance, what does that word truly mean? Second, ask yourself what that gift/asset does for you? How does it benefit you? And last, but not least, how does this gift affect others in a beautiful way? Going through these steps with your final three words can be a powerful gratitude exercise.

The Choice is Always (Authentically) Yours.

Perhaps the dog really did eat your homework or you got passed up for a promotion. So what? You can control your life just as much as you can control your calendar. Things don't happen to you — you're the driver and it's up to you to make things happen. It is much easier to blame circumstances and others for our downfalls or mistakes, but the truth is, the choice is ours. We are in control of our mindset, our actions and our success — believe you can, and you will.

When I look back at my life, I'd like to think I would have done it "my way" on every level. And that starts with understanding who I am at the core and eliminating any noise that stands in my way. Yes, committing to personal growth and uncovering your true self is no easy feat. It takes courage, curiosity, patience and discipline. And there are setbacks along the way. There were times I doubted the value and nearly threw in the towel. But as with anything, sticking to the goal and committing to personal mastery can bring more beauty to life than ever imagined.

As one of my good friends, the Skin Horse in the original Velveteen Rabbit book, once said:

"It doesn't happen all at once. You become. It takes a long time. That's why it doesn't happen often to people who break easily, or have sharp edges, or who have to carefully be kept. Generally, by the time you are Real, most of your hair has been loved off, and your eyes drop out and you get loose in the joints and very shabby. But these things don't matter at all, because once you are Real you can't be ugly, except to people who don't understand."

I hope you enjoy your journey to authenticity as much as I have.

About the Author

Anna Crowe is founder and CEO of Crowe PR, a best-selling author, podcaster and speaker. In addition to running her award-winning public relations and marketing agency and empowering people to unlock their true potential through authenticity, Anna spends her time supporting and inspiring others around her. She is an active board member at the San Diego Chapter of the Entrepreneurs' Organization, philanthropy-based PEERS Network and digital wellness non-profit Half The Story, volunteering her time helping small businesses and non-profit organizations.

Anna's focus on developing extraordinary leaders and growing her clients' businesses has led to several notable recognitions, including CEO of the Year, Best Places to Work, PR Team of the Year, Women Who Mean Busines and more. Anna holds an MBA in International Marketing from the University of San Diego and a bachelor's degree in Accounting from Rutgers University. She is fulfilled when she positively impacts another human being, grows as an individual and a leader, travels the world with her family, and catches a coastal sunset, with a glass of Pinot Noir.

Connect With Anna:

www.CrowePR.com
LinkedIn: annacrowe25
Instagram: @acrowepr

CHAPTER 10

HELP is a Four-Letter Word

By Lauren Reed

I HAD BEEN HIKING UP A MOUNTAIN in Africa for five straight days with a group of fellow business owners. I started to experience altitude sickness around day two and it was getting progressively worse. It was summit night and I had been throwing up right outside my tent for hours. Our plan was to leave base camp at midnight to reach the summit of Mount Kilimanjaro by sunrise.

I somehow got myself ready and stumbled over to meet the rest of my group. I knew as soon as I saw their faces that I looked as bad as I felt. Our guide gently urged me back down the mountain. My oxygen levels were dropping, and it wasn't safe for me to join the group on our summit bid.

I was devastated. I had set a goal to climb the world's largest freestanding mountain — putting in the training, flying across the world, and hiking for five straight days only to fail at achieving my goal with one final hike left.

At the time, I thought this was the worst thing that could ever happen to me. By all accounts, I had a fantastic life. My PR and marketing agency, founded in 2012, had quickly grown to reach the desirable million-dollar mark, which opened up a world of possibilities and opportunities that I had never even imagined. I truly loved my team and the work we did with national and global brands.

I had two healthy and beautiful children, a stable marriage, and an amazing support network of friends and fellow business owners. I regularly ran marathons and 50km races. I prided myself on being able to accomplish big goals, both personally and professionally, which is why I was truly crushed that I didn't complete what I had set out to do.

You see, while I seemingly had it all under control, there was one piece of advice I had continually been given that I just couldn't seem to grasp, and my inability to do so was making my life exponentially more difficult.

ASK FOR HELP.

Yes, it sounds simple. However, my fierce independence and pride often stood in the way, and life was about to give me the exact experiences I needed to work through this challenge.

It turned out that all I had to do was wait a few more months and suddenly, not summitting a mountain didn't seem like such a big deal anymore.

Let's fast forward.

***

It was my first week as a single mother.

I was lying in bed recovering from surgery, unable to walk or drive, with multiple physical therapist and doctor's appointments each week.

I was sick to my stomach, and it still isn't clear if it was from the loads of antibiotics the doctors were feeding me, or the mere thought that I was letting everyone down.

The backstory is that a recent trip ended in a pretty gnarly ski accident. It was the final straw in a series of events that forced me — a very strong-willed and some might say stubborn — entrepreneur to realize that I am not invincible, and I actually do need other people.

In the past several months, I had also lost 40% of my business during the first two weeks of the COVID-19 pandemic.

While focusing on saving my company, like many of you, I had two children who suddenly needed to be homeschooled.

And my 15-year marriage, the relationship I had been in since I was 18-years-old, fell apart, leaving me full of a grief that I refused to acknowledge.

I was in pain from my surgery, but if I am being honest, the thing that hurt the most was my already-broken spirit.

It turned out to be exactly what I needed, and what forced me to finally absorb what it means to be in a completely vulnerable place and really ask for help.

You see, I knew the power of community from a business perspective, but I didn't treat my personal life the same way. Lying there in my dark room, I realized that the reason my business made it through the pandemic is because I asked for help.

With the help of my peers and mentors, I navigated the world of paycheck protection (PPP) money, strategized a new line of revenue, and looked at every inch of my financials to determine how long I could afford to keep my full team employed. Because I asked for help, we had double-digit revenue growth during a pandemic. I kept my entire team employed and was even able to make a couple of new hires when small businesses all around me were dealing with furloughs and layoffs.

I did not hesitate to pull out all the stops when it came to making sure my company made it through the pandemic. But during this same timeframe, I was unwinding my marriage, and I didn't treat my personal life with the same intention as my business. The Universe intervened, as it does, to give me the exact experiences I needed to move past my fears.

You know, I have noticed a trend with business leaders. Most of us are comfortable asking for help with our companies. The problem is, as entrepreneurs, we don't always treat our personal lives as well as we treat our businesses, and there is a reason for that — it is scary stuff!

Let's think about this. Do you feel that you have someone who you can call at 4 am and they will be there for you, no questions asked? These are your ride-or-die folks. Maybe it is family. For me, it is a group of dear girlfriends.

Most people respond to this question with an emphatic, "Yes!" However, when I follow up by asking if they are comfortable actually being the one to make that call at 4 am to ask for help, the discomfort is typically pretty obvious.

I believe that as entrepreneurs, we should apply the same approach that we use with our businesses to our personal lives, and in this chapter, I will share the actionable steps I took using principles learned in business that finally helped me move past my fear of asking for help outside of work. The result? I can now experience the joy of letting others in and truly living in community.

PART ONE:

The first step I took was really identifying my resistance to asking for help.

While I had to do this in the midst of a crisis, I encourage you to do this now. In this life, we don't have the luxury of knowing when the next moment that will knock us down will come, and if this is an area you struggle with, let's begin the work right away and practice while the stakes are still low.

Personally, I had a ton of reasons not to ask for help, and they played in a constant loop in my head.

Lauren, you cannot ask someone to drive you to the doctor in the middle of the workday. Time is money! You know this.

You see, my entire career I have billed by the quarter-hour. I know the value of time, and in an industry like mine, it is one of your most valuable assets.

Lauren, you should be able to figure this out. Don't bother other people with YOUR problems. They have their own stuff to deal with.

I am strong! I can handle things on my own.

Lauren, for goodness sake — you don't want to appear too needy.

I have always prided myself on my ability to be highly productive and independent. What would this say about me?

There is a ton of research from experts about how to overcome fears such is this. Hypnosis. Long-term therapy. Reprogramming your brain.

And I do believe those are all viable options — just not the most practical when you are lying in bed trying to figure out how you will make it to a physiotherapy appointment the very next day.

When you find yourself in a constant loop of resistance, put pen to paper and write it down. Jot down whatever comes to mind when I suggest you ask for help.

Now let's sit with it for a moment. Identify any common themes. Take a hard look at WHY you are afraid to ask for help. And while you do this, recognize how your body reacts. For me, even just sharing these statements can take me right back to that sick feeling — of knots in my stomach.

You might not have an immediate answer and that is OK!

It took me a good amount of reflection to realize that my fear of asking for help was actually a fear of rejection, and this came from self-esteem issues stemming all the way back to childhood. I was worried that people wouldn't have time to give, and a very vulnerable part of me worried that even if they did, they wouldn't want to spend it on me.

And if I didn't put myself out there to ask, I wouldn't get hurt, right? Here's the kicker. I thought I had already done this work. I mean, I follow Brené Brown!

Seriously, though, bouts of anxiety throughout my twenties and early thirties led me to therapy where a lot of deep healing occurred. But healing is an ongoing process, and I am certainly a work in progress. I really had to stop and figure out why some deep-rooted issues were manifesting in this way now.

There was more work to be done, and what do we do as entrepreneurs who see a problem? We create. I developed a long-term roadmap to not just managing but overcoming this issue.

PART TWO:

The second thing we will discuss is how to identify where you need help.

My immediate issue was clear — I needed car rides! But my hesitancy to ask for help on that one thing was an indicator of how I handled all of my relationships, and I needed a process to get better at this.

I was reminded of a time about a year prior. My daughter was turning four and she came to me with a birthday present request, as kids do.

"Mommy, I know what I want for my birthday this year! I want all-by-myself-lessons," she requested.

I looked at her, confused.

"What do you mean, Annie?" I asked.

"Well, I want to be able to do everything by myself so I never have to ask anyone for help. You know, like Jack [her brother] takes guitar and swimming lessons," she explained.

I am going to be brutally honest right now. I wish I had taken that statement more seriously. Instead, I laughed it off and was proud of her independence. She is MY daughter, after all.

I tell this story to remind you that there is a small window of time to improve our communications in the relationships that matter the most. As entrepreneurs and leaders within our companies, our behavior is constantly being watched, whether we realize it or not. In this case, it was my daughter at home who was learning from me to not bother others with her needs.

But it just as easily could be one of my employees. Think about it — when someone on your team is dealing with a difficult issue, do you want them to feel they have to handle it independently? Or would you prefer they alert you so that you can help solve the problem?

"But Lauren, we have an open-door policy!" you say. "My team knows they can come to me!"

Maybe so. And look, I know this is a fine line.

How we act and behave will impact our personal and professional relationships — and if I am saying one thing at the office but they are watching me refuse to ask for help personally, what am I REALLY saying?

When I shared this in a talk with a couple of dozen local business owners, it clearly struck a nerve. For weeks, I received feedback that this is a real struggle. Each email I opened, I was humbled and felt less alone — and found myself more determined than ever to learn and grow from this challenge.

Now that I am on a newfound mission to leave that silo — where I felt I had to do all and be all to everyone without needing anything from anyone — I have found it helpful to use some of the tools we have learned in business settings to gut-check that my behaviors are, in fact, aligned with this goal. Through my involvement with Entrepreneurs' Organization (EO), I am in a forum of seven business owners that meet every month. Our forums are a safe place where we have been trained to open up and share the things we cannot talk about with 95% of the world.

Let's be real — not everyone in your life knows what it feels like to have the weight of the world on your shoulders. Like the fear that you may not make payroll because clients are slow-paying during a global pandemic, potentially impacting your twelve employees and their families. We need our forums for this reason!

And while it felt radical, I desired to build upon the work I was doing in my forum to begin practicing this in other areas of my life.

To me, my forum is a very safe space. I am already in a radically honest mindset when it comes to my business when I am prepping for our monthly meetings. I realized that I could take advantage of this mindset by allocating a few extra minutes of reflection to look at my relationships and life OUTSIDE my forum to identify the areas where I need help. So, I developed a worksheet designed to do a quick brain dump in areas of my life where I needed support.

I am a sucker for writing things down, and when I set a goal on paper, I tend to keep it. In addition to normalizing the need for community in my life, this simple exercise has helped alleviate my fear of asking for help from others.

PART THREE:

Finally, how do you actually make the ask?

This is hard stuff! It still baffles me that by most accounts, people consider me a strong person. I can run a successful business, yet the mere thought of asking someone for a car ride gives me sheer anxiety.

While working through this process with my EO forum, we had some pretty raw dialogue about this. In the past several months, two other members also had pretty severe medical emergencies.

We all shared our reasons for shying away from asking for help when put in that position — some were the same, some were different. As I mentioned, this is really an inside job and how you respond really depends on your background. But we came to the same conclusion.

When we finally DID ask for help, people were honored to step in. Think about it — I am always happy to support others. In fact, it brings me immense joy when someone turns to me and strengthens our connection. In a way, by trying to maintain the independence that I had grown to be so proud of, I was essentially withholding this joy from others.

Now, this realization certainly helped push me to make the ask, but it didn't make the process any less clumsy. I still felt awkward and hesitant. I have found that there are three concrete things to consider when asking for help.

Clarity is key – be very specific about how someone can help and what you need. For me, it was car rides to a specific place at specific times. By removing the ambiguity, it makes it easier for people to respond, and you will actually get the help that you need.

Don't apologize. This was a hard one for me! "I'm so sorry but do you mind…" or "I hate to ask this but…" Remove all of those qualifiers and just sincerely ask for what you need.

Actually listen and accept the help! In my experience, before I went down this road, people would often offer to help but I would shoo their offers away. But it is different when you are the one making the ask, so be prepared to humbly and gratefully let someone in. My natural inclination, even after someone accepted my request for help, is to ask, "Are you sure?" or "I can figure it out if you can't." Crazy, right? I ask someone for what I need. They give it to me. I then try to talk them out of it? What kind of sense does that make?

It really doesn't, and just goes to show that lifelong patterns are hard to break, and you have to keep practicing.

I'll close by sharing my actual experience of asking for help.

Lying there in bed, I posted on Facebook that I needed help to get to physical therapy and doctor's appointments for at least the next month. It was super uncomfortable for me.

I posted anyways because I was desperate. Within 24 hours, more than 100 people contacted me to offer their help. I was stunned. Most of them didn't even know that I had undergone surgery. You see, when I struggle, I tend to do it very privately and only share something difficult that has happened once I make it through and have a smile back on my face.

The car rides lasted for nearly two months. Around 20 minutes each way, 40 minutes total, at least three times a week.

When is the last time I had 120 minutes a week of focused time with people who cared enough about me to give up their time to drive me to and from my appointments? No one asked me about my business or needed anything from me. I wasn't Lauren, owner of REED PR. I was just a girl, recovering from surgery, learning to walk again.

These car rides gave me renewed hope and valuable time to really connect with people who really love me and wanted to help. Asking for help taught me how to be in the moment and allow happiness into my life, even when it felt like everything was crumbling down around me.

My challenge to you is to take the best practices you have learned in business and apply them to your personal lives, just as well as you do in your businesses.

Asking for help is a sign of strength. It is true in your business, and it is true in your personal life.

About the Author

Lauren Reed, APR is the president and founder of REED Public Relations. She earned her Accreditation in Public Relations designation in 2010 and has been a long-standing member of the Public Relations Society of America, serving as president of the Nashville chapter in 2017.

Lauren is a member of the Women Presidents' Organization and serves on the board for the Entrepreneurs' Organization.

Lauren has also been named to the Nashville Business Journal's 40 Under 40 and its list of Most Admired CEOs in 2018, 2019, 2020 and 2021. She also received a Nashville Emerging Leader Award from the Nashville Area Chamber of Commerce. Most recently, Lauren was named to the Nashville Post's InCharge list and has been featured in publications such as StyleBlueprint, Bizwomen and The New York Times.

Alongside REED PR's partner and co-founder, Katie Adkisson, Lauren has led the agency to double digit percentage growth each year since it was founded. Lauren also spearheaded the agency's internal give-back program, Be The Good, which uses a portion of annual profits to fund service trips both locally and abroad. Last year, Lauren and Katie led the development of REED's COVID-19 Communications Hotline, which provided free PR and marketing counsel to small business owners during the pandemic.

Connect with Lauren:

www.ReedPublicRelations.com
lauren@reedpublicrelations.com
Instagram: @reed_pr

EPILOGUE

"Strong women don't have attitude.
They have standards and boundaries."
– Andrea Heuston

I wrote that line as the intro quote of an article that was published in December of 2019. The article, *Never Apologize for Being a Strong Woman,* went viral. Women saw it as a rallying cry to stop trying to be what we're not, and to embrace what and who we are.

I believe that female leaders can rub people the wrong way with their straightforward approach to life. Most of us have a background that has created a need to be gritty, tenacious, and passionate in a way that some people take offense to. Many of us have been interpreted as demanding or even bossy. But the truth is that strong women can also be very sensitive and thoughtful.

When we Lead Like Women, we demonstrate a belief in ourselves, in our worth, and in our own point of view. I encourage you to Lead Like a Woman in all areas of your life. Understand and know your worth, even when it feels like a stretch to get there. Do not rely on others' opinions of your life; your decisions and your journey are yours alone and they've created the person you are now, the person you'll become in the future.

Please join us on this journey through owning our stories and forging ourselves in fire. This book is the first in a series of *Lead Like a Woman* books. I'm excited to share these stories with you about women who have overcome, learned, and led with grace and style.

I'm proud to Lead Like a Woman. I'm proud to be strong. I hope you are too.

See you soon!

Book Club Questions

Some of the most impactful discussions I have ever had have been around a table or a friend's living room while sipping beverages and eating snacks with other women. "Lead Like a Woman: Tales From the Trenches" is perfect for such a discussion!

The best book clubs encourage all voices to participate. Gather everyone in a large space and have a blast discussing everyone's thoughts and experiences with the book. Use the following questions to inspire conversation.

1. Were any of the stories in the book surprising?

2. What did you find inspiring about this book?

3. What was your biggest takeaway from the book?

4. What is the most important piece of advice offered in this book?

5. Who would you recommend this book to?

6. What did you like most about the book?

7. What did you like least about the book?

8. What is the significance of the title? Would you have given the book a different title?

9. Have you ever dealt with a similar situation to any of the situations in the book?

10. If you got the chance to ask one of the authors of this book one question, which author would you ask and what would your question be?

Made in United States
North Haven, CT
26 May 2022

19561498R00102